Real Estate

ESSENTIALS

Real Estate

ESSENTIALS

A Glossary and Study Guide

LearningExpress,
with Ralph Tamper, Ed Farthing,
Pat Farthing, and Mary Masi

New York

Library of Congress Cataloging-in-Publication Data:
Real estate essentials a glossary and study guide / Ralph Tamper, Pat Farthing and Ed Farthing with Mary Masi.
    p. cm.
  ISBN 1-57685-412-4
  1. Real estate business—United States—States—Examinations, questions, etc.—Study guides. 2. Real estate business—Licenses—United States—States—Examinations, questions, etc.—Study guides. 3. Real estate agents—Licenses—United States—States—Examinations, questions, etc.—Study guides. 4. Real estate business—Law and legislation—United States—States—Examinations, questions, etc.—Study guides. 5. Real property—United States—States—Examinations, questions, etc.—Study guides. 6. Real estate business—United States—States—Terminology. I. Tamper, Ralph.
  HD1381 .R387 2002
  333.33'9873—dc21

               2002003295

Printed in the United States of America
9 8 7 6 5 4 3 2 1
First Edition

ISBN 1-57685-412-4

For more information or to place an order, contact LearningExpress at:
  900 Broadway
  Suite 604
  New York, NY 10003

Or visit us at:
  www.learnatest.com

About the Authors

Ralph Tamper is a nationally recognized authority in the real estate field as educator, trainer, and author. He was President of the Real Estate Education Association, 2001–2002, and a Member of National Association of REALTORS® Education Committee, 2000–2001. He has written on subjects such as real estate mathematics and real estate contracts, and he is an advisor on a guide to real estate sales, *Closing the Deal*.

Edward C. Farthing is a licensed broker for 28 years and a licensed salesperson for 33 years. He is licensed in both New York and Pennsylvania, and has sold, leased, built, renovated, appraised, and managed property throughout the region.

Patricia B. Farthing is a licensed Real Estate Broker in Broome County, New York. She has been a broker for the past 16 years and a licensed salesperson for 24 years. Pat and Ed Farthing are Associate Brokers with Coldwell Banker in Broome County, New York. Also, they are expert panelists on *The Unofficial Guide to Buying a Home* and advisors on *Closing the Deal*.

Mary Masi is an editorial consultant at InfoSurge, Inc. in Sunrise, Florida.

Contents

Real Estate

ESSENTIALS

Chapter **1**

How to Use this Book to Get a Top Score

*I*f you are planning to take a real estate licensing exam, this book can help you to get a top score on your test. It will show you how to put all the pieces of test preparation together. You can use this book as a study guide and methodically work your way through it from cover to cover—from learning new study strategies and memory tricks, to using the terms in the glossary to create flash cards and study lists. Or, if you have already passed your real estate exam, you can use this book as a reference to help you throughout your real estate career.

YOUR UPCOMING REAL ESTATE EXAM

In most states, you will be required to pass a written test to become licensed as a real estate sales person or broker. However, the specific exam you will be required to take depends on the state in which you want to become licensed. If you aren't sure which real estate exam you need to take, contact the real estate commission in the state in which you wish to be licensed for detailed information on their specific licensing requirements.

Some states administer their own examination for prospective real estate licensees, such as California. Other states use the services of an independent testing company. Four of the most commonly used independent testing companies are listed below, along with their contact information.

Assessment Systems, Inc. (ASI)
3 Bala Plaza West, Suite 300
Bala Cynwyd, PA 19004-3481
610-618-2565
www.asisvcs.com

Psychological Services, Inc. (PSI)
100 West Broadway, Suite 1100
Glendale, CA 91210-1202
800-RE-EXAMS (800-733-9267)

Applied Measurement Professionals, Inc. (AMP)
8310 Neiman Road
Lenexa, KS 66214
800-345-6559 or 913-541-0400
www.goamp.com

Experior Assessments, LLC
1360 Energy Park Drive
St. Paul, MN 55108
651-647-1723
www.experioronline.com

The real estate exams used by these independent testing companies to examine prospective real estate professionals are in a multiple-choice question format, as are most state administered real estate exams. Here's a sample breakdown of the typical topics and approximate number of multiple-choice questions in each topic for the real estate written exams administered by these four testing companies. Keep in mind that some states vary the total number of questions asked in each topic, and will also have state-specific questions added to the national exam for use in their state. For example, in Michigan an additional 30 questions that relate specifically to Michigan state laws and rules are included on the real estate licensing exam administered by AMP.

AMP	Number of Questions
Listing Property	25
Selling Property	20
Property Management	10
Settlement/Transfer of Ownership	14
Financing	21
Professional Responsibilities/Fair Practice/ Administration	10
TOTAL QUESTIONS ON THE NATIONAL PORTION OF THE TEST	**100**

PSI	Number of Questions
Property Ownership	10
Land Use Controls and Regulations	8
Valuation and Market Analysis	6
Financing	10
Laws of Agency	9
Mandated Disclosures	3
Contracts	10
Transfer of Property	6
Practice	6
Real Estate Mathematics	9
Specialty Areas	3
TOTAL QUESTIONS ON THE NATIONAL PORTION OF THE TEST	**80**

ASI	Number of Questions
Real Property Characteristics, Definitions, Ownership, Restrictions, and Transfer	16
Assessing and Explaining Property Valuation and the Appraisal Process	12
Contracts, Agency Relationships with Buyers and Sellers, and Federal Requirements	20
Financing the Transaction and Settlement	20
Leases, Rents, and Property Management	12
TOTAL QUESTIONS ON THE NATIONAL PORTION OF THE TEST	**80**

EXPERIOR	Number of Questions
Business Practices and Ethics	12
Agency and Listing	12
Property Characteristics, Descriptions, Ownership, Interests, and Restrictions	12
Property Valuation and the Appraisal Process	8
Real Estate Sales Contracts	12
Financing Sources	8
Property Management	4
Closing/Settlement and Transferring Title	12
TOTAL QUESTIONS ON THE NATIONAL PORTION OF THE TEST	**80**

Regardless of whether you take a state-administered real estate exam or one administered by AMP, PSI, ASI, or Experior, you will need to know the same basic real estate information. That is why this book can help you no matter which state you want to become licensed in. You will need to know the real estate terms included in the glossary of this book for all the different real estate licensing exams out there. The study skills sections will also help you no matter which specific real estate licensing exam you are required to take.

HOW THIS BOOK CAN HELP YOU

The entire process of preparing for a real estate exam, which may seem overwhelming at first glance, can actually be broken down into several manageable steps. This book guides you through each of those steps. The first step is to finish orienting yourself with this introductory chapter. Then, move on to Chapter 2, which explains how to set up an individualized study plan and presents specific study strategies you can use during your study sessions. You will find out the steps to take in order to maximize your chances for scoring high on your upcoming exam. You will find out when to take sample tests so you can check your scores and still have enough time to focus on the areas in which you need more work. You will also increase your understanding and retention of the real estate material you are studying by using many different study strategies, not just one or two.

While you are reading Chapter 2, take the time to create an individualized study plan that will fit your needs and schedule. This is a crucial step in the test-preparation process. Also, be sure to take at least one practice exam online or from a real estate test preparation book, as recommended in the sample study plan. After you finish reading Chapter 2, spend some time using each different study strategy explained in that chapter.

Chapter 3 will show you how to create, use, organize, and review mnemonic devices, which are memory tricks that can help you to overcome memory blocks during a real estate exam. Mnemonics such as *acronyms* and *acrostics* can help you score extra points by helping you to remember lists and terms when you need to. As you will find out from reading Chapter 3, mnemonics are best used *after* you have become familiar with specific real estate material—they should not be used to try and learn brand new material.

After you finish reading Chapter 3, it's time to tackle the glossary section, which makes up the bulk of this book. The glossary contains a wealth of essential real estate terms that you will either be learning for the first time or reviewing. If you are new to the real estate field, this glossary of terms may become the backbone of your study sessions. You will need to learn, or at least become familiar with most of the terms in this section of the book. If you already have some experience as a real estate professional, this portion of the book will be a valuable reference and review tool for you.

USE THIS BOOK WITH OTHER TEST-PREPARATION MATERIAL

This book is best used along with test preparation books or websites that allow you to take practice real estate exams. *Real Estate Essentials* fills an important gap left by many test-preparation books because they do not contain a thorough glossary of terms. Additionally, most test-preparation books do not explain specific study strategies or show how mnemonic devices can help you remember difficult terminology.

If you are committed to becoming a real estate professional, you should also invest the time and money into buying and using a test-preparation book that includes several practice real estate exams, or log onto the Web to take practice exams so that you get the best of both types of study material. Put them together, and you have a winning combination that can help you get a top score on your exam. See Chapter 2 for specific guidance on how to fit practice exams into your study schedule. You will find a variety of test-preparation books at your local bookstore or library, or you can order them online. Here are some suggested test-preparation books:

PSI Exam

PSI Real Estate Sales Exam: The Complete Preparation Guide
(book includes free CD-ROM). LearningExpress, 1998.

AMP Exam

AMP Real Estate Sales Exam: The Complete Preparation Guide
(book includes free CD-ROM). LearningExpress, 1998.

ASI Exam

ASI Real Estate Sales Exam: The Complete Preparation Guide
(book includes free CD-ROM). LearningExpress, 1998.

Texas State Exam

*Texas Real Estate Sales Exam: The Complete Preparation Guide
2nd Edition.* (book includes free CD-ROM). Learning-
Express, 2000.

California State Exam

*California Real Estate Sales Exam: The Complete Preparation
Guide.* LearningExpress, 1999.

Florida State Exam

Florida Real Estate Exam Manual. David S. Coleman, et al.
Dearborn Trade, 2000.

In addition, the Internet contains a wealth of test-
preparation resources for real estate exams. Some sites even offer
online practice exams, complete with answer explanations, per-
sonalized scoring, and individual analysis. Many real estate exams
are now computer-based, meaning that when you go to take the
exam, you will take it on a computer. Therefore, online practice
tests are not only a valuable learning tool, but they can also help

you become familiar with and feel prepared for the official test come test day. Check out the website LearnATest.com to take practice real estate exams online.

After reading and studying this book and taking several practice real estate exams, you will be well on your way to getting a top score on your upcoming real estate exam. Good luck as you enter or further your exciting and rewarding real estate career!

Chapter 2

Studying For Success

Successful studying for a real estate exam is a skill that you can master. This chapter will show you how to create a study plan and will give you several different strategies you can use to make the most of each study session as you prepare for your upcoming real estate exam.

The first step to successful studying is to set up a study plan. In other words, take a few minutes to create a study schedule for yourself. This will allow you to get an overview of what you need to accomplish, and it will help you to establish interim deadlines throughout your study schedule. The time you spend developing a study plan will serve you well as you prepare for your upcoming exam.

Take a moment to think about your goal. Most likely, your goal is to pass a specific real estate licensing examination. So let's work backward from that end result of passing your exam. How much time do you have? Can you plan a leisurely schedule of study for several months, or do you need to cover a lot of material in just a few weeks or less?

An important aspect of a study plan is flexibility. Your plan should help you, not hinder you, so be prepared to alter your study schedule once you get started, if necessary. You will probably find that one or more steps will take longer to complete than you had anticipated, while others will go more quickly.

CREATING YOUR STUDY PLAN

The following sample study plan can give you an idea of how to create your own individualized study schedule. Each step of your plan should be flexible, but you can use this timeline as a guide. If you have more time, you can expand the plan; if you have less time, you can compress it.

Sample Study Plan

This schedule is appropriate if you have approximately four to six months before your real estate examination test date.

Four to Six Months before the Test

1. Read Chapters 1–3 of this book.
2. Request all materials needed for your test.
3. Buy a large calendar and mark the date of your test on it. Highlight or clearly emphasize the date with a bright color pen so it stands out every time you glance at the calendar.
4. Select a real estate test-preparation book or online test-prep site that contains sample real estate exams

that you can take for practice. Titles of suggested books and online resources are listed in Chapter 1.

5. Take a practice test either online or from your test-preparation book and carefully check your score. Note how you performed on the different topics appearing on the test. Create a simple chart that has ample room to record several test scores. Save this chart so you can log each of your practice test scores on it.

6. Get in the habit of studying your real estate textbooks every day. It's better to study 20 minutes every day of the week than to save up all those minutes and cram several hours of study into one day on the weekend. By breaking up your study time, you're more apt to remember the material.

7. Experiment by using the different study strategies discussed in this chapter. Perhaps you want to try a different one each week. Then, if you find that one method works especially well for you, you can use that method for more of your study sessions.

Two to Three Months before the Test

1. Set aside a specific amount of time each day to review test areas you need to concentrate on to improve your score. Even if you can only squeeze in 15–20 minutes a day, those minutes add up over the course of a week and can dramatically improve your knowledge. Continue using a variety of study strategies during your study sessions.

2. Take another practice test either online or from a real estate test-preparation book. Record your score on the graph or chart you created. Are your scores steadily going up or are they uneven? Note which type of questions you got wrong so you can review those areas.

3. Try to enlist the help of a friend or relative who will quiz you on important words and concepts you are studying. Your friend can use the glossary in this book to quiz you on a variety of terms and their definitions.

One Month before the Test

1. Confirm the date and location of your exam.

2. Confirm that your application to take the exam has been received and that you have been sent all the necessary materials.

3. Make sure you know where the test will be held and how you will get to the test site.

4. Continue to spend at least 15 minutes every day studying and reviewing real estate material. If you can manage to spend more time in review sessions each day, that is even better. However, if you have been reviewing regularly for a couple of months, the reviews should take you less time since you are now so familiar with the material. This is the most important part of studying for tests. The more familiar you are with the information that will be on the test, the better you will perform under testing conditions.

5. Seek support and encouragement from those closest to you. If you live with others, remind them that you have an important test coming up and you need quiet time to study.

One Week before the Test

1. Take two more practice tests either online or from a real estate test-prep book. See how your scores compare with the tests you took at the beginning of your study plan. Try not to become anxious if your score is lower than you think it should be at this point. The reality is that you *do* know more than when you started studying, and it will show when you actually take the test.

2. Concentrate on being well rested and relaxed about taking the test. Avoid stress and anxiety as much as possible. Each time you find yourself worrying about the test, say to yourself, "I am well prepared and I will do well on this test." Remember, you have been studying hard for the past several months, using this book and other real estate test-prep material; if you have been keeping to your study plan, you should be prepared for your test. Thinking positive thoughts each day can help prepare you mentally for doing well on the test.

3. Continue your daily study sessions. Even if you feel that you already understand all of the material, you can spend time reviewing and creating mnemonics (you will learn more about mnemonics in the next chapter).

4. Make sure you have all necessary items—pencils, watch, a sweater, and so on—and that you have arranged for plenty of time to get to the test site.

Don't Be Tempted to Cram

By creating a study plan, you can avoid the panic of cramming. Trying frantically to learn all the material you need to know the night before your big exam can frazzle your nerves and leave you too exhausted to do your best on test day.

STUDY STRATEGIES YOU CAN USE

After you develop a study plan, the next step to successful studying is to decide what specific things you want to do during your study sessions. Using a variety of study strategies rather than simply reading and rereading your real estate textbooks can help you make the material come alive so that you thoroughly understand it. You can also avoid boredom during your study sessions by using many different study methods.

Try using a different study strategy each time you sit down to study, or you could use a variety of study strategies throughout the day. For example, rewrite some of your notes in the morning, carry flash cards along with you during the day for those times when you find that you have a few free minutes, and create some sample study questions during your evening study session.

Some study strategies will appeal to you more than others. However, give each strategy a chance by trying it at least once, because even if it doesn't seem appealing at first, you might be surprised by how much it can help you learn. The rest of this chapter describes specific study strategies you can use. Each strategy can help you understand and remember the material you need to know to ace your upcoming real estate exam.

Asking Questions

Asking questions is a powerful study strategy because it forces you to get actively involved in the material you want to learn. Getting actively involved will help you to better understand and remember that material when test time comes around. Another benefit of asking questions is that you may end up asking (and then answering) some of the very same questions that will appear on your exam.

Here are some sample questions you can ask yourself while reading and reviewing your real estate textbooks:

1. What is the main idea from this section?
2. How does the information in this section relate to other information I already know?
3. What are the key terms in this section that I should memorize?
4. What are the facts from this section that I need to know for the exam?
5. How can I turn these facts into questions?

Of course, not all of the questions you ask about the material you are studying will appear on an exam; however, you will find that many of your questions will at least be related to information tested on the exam. It is much better to ask and answer specific questions than to aimlessly read and reread a textbook without any goal in mind.

If you're having trouble coming up with questions based on the material you are studying, get out a test-preparation book that contains sample real estate exams and read through several of the questions. The more practice tests you take, the more familiar you will become with the types of questions you can form from your material.

To give you an idea of how to create specific questions regarding material you are reading, take a look at the sample questions that follow this passage:

> The Federal Fair Housing laws prohibit discrimination in housing because of race or color, national origin, religion, sex, familial status (including children under the age of 18 living with parents or legal custodians, pregnant women, and people securing custody of children under 18), or handicap. The Fair Housing laws cover most housing. In some circumstances, however, the law exempts owner-occupied buildings with no more than four units, single-family housing sold or rented without the use of a broker, and housing operated by organizations and private clubs that limit occupancy to members.
>
> Furthermore, in the sale and rental of housing, no one may take any of the following actions based on race, color, national origin, religion, sex, familial status, or handicap:
> - refuse to rent or sell housing
> - refuse to negotiate for housing
> - make housing unavailable
> - deny a dwelling

- set different terms, conditions, or privileges for sale or rental of a dwelling
- provide different housing services or facilities
- falsely deny that housing is available for inspection, sale, or rental
- for profit, persuade owners to sell or rent (block-busting)
- deny anyone access to, or membership in, a facility or service (such as a multiple listing service) related to the sale or rental of housing

Sample Questions
1. What would be a good title for this passage?
2. What groups of people are included in the term *familial status*?
3. True or False: The Federal Housing laws apply to all types of housing.
4. What is the main idea of this passage?

By asking questions about the material you read, you help cement into your mind the facts and ideas contained in that material. You can even go a step further and actually come up with multiple-choice questions. Your multiple-choice questions can be adapted from questions you've already asked yourself about the material, or they can cover new topics. Creating multiple-choice questions gives you the chance to step into the role of a teacher (or test developer) and actually practice coming up with a correct answer in the face of several distracters (the other answer choices that are incorrect). Here's an example of the type of multiple-choice questions you could create based on the questions asked above:

1. Which of the following would be the best title for this passage?
    a. "Housing Problems in America"
    b. "The Fair Housing Bill of 1990"
    c. "Federal Fair Housing Laws"
    d. "Americans With Disabilities Act"

2. The term *familial status* includes the following groups of people EXCEPT:
    a. children under the age of 18 living with parents or legal custodians.
    b. pregnant women.
    c. people securing custody of children under 18.
    d. people securing custody of children over 18.

3. In which case would an owner be exempt from the Fair Housing laws?
    a. An owner of a building containing five dwelling units as long as the owner lives in one of the units
    b. An owner of a commercial property
    c. An owner of a building constructed before 1991
    d. An owner of a building containing three dwelling units as long as the owner lives in one of the units

4. Which of the following best expresses the main idea of the passage?
    a. Property owners should not discriminate against people who have disabilities.
    b. Real estate professionals should always carry with them a copy of the Fair Housing Laws.

c. The Federal Fair Housing Laws prohibit discrimination on the basis of race, color, religion, national origin, sex, familial status, or handicap.

d. People tend to discriminate against others in the real estate field.

Now comes the fun part: answering the questions! (The answers for the above questions are: 1. **c**, 2. **d**, 3. **d**, 4. **c**.) By the time you've gone through the process of developing questions based on a section of material you want to learn, you will probably already have a good idea of what the answers are. However, it's always a good idea to read through your questions to see if you can answer them without having to look back at the material. You can use your list of questions each time you want to review the material. If time permits, you can also ask additional questions during your review of the material.

To organize your questions, you can either put all your written questions in a separate place, such as a three-ring binder, folder, or notebook, or you can include them alongside your notes in a notebook that you use in class or while studying your texts. One way to organize your questions so you can use them later as a review tool is to write down your questions and answers on sheets of paper that you can fold in half. Then, write your questions on the left side and brief answers on the right side. That way, you can fold the paper with the answers underneath to quiz yourself.

After you ask and answer several questions about a topic you are studying, set the questions aside for a few days. Then, without looking at the answers, ask yourself the same questions again and see how many you can answer correctly. Write down additional questions as they come to mind during your review. Often, your search for the answers to your questions will lead to more questions. However, the more questions you ask, the more answers you will find, and the more material you will know on exam day.

Taking Notes

Taking notes in class or on what you read will help you to understand and remember the information you need to know on exam day. Proper note taking develops your thinking skills. It can help you to listen better, organize material, and recall, digest, and interpret information.

The secret to taking good notes is knowing what is important enough to write down—and what is not. Three things that are important enough to record are:

1. Main ideas and secondary ideas
2. Authorities
3. Opinions and facts

If you are taking a real estate course, make it a priority to listen closely for main points during each lecture. Learn to separate the main points from the minor, or supporting, ones. A good instructor will identify main points for you, but sometimes you have to do this on your own. Here are some verbal clues instructors may use that point toward a main or important idea:

> the reason is . . .
> an important factor . . .
> there are four things to consider . . .

the thing to remember . . .

the best (or worse, biggest, smallest, last, only, and so on) . . .

Secondary ideas are often buried in examples, so be alert to this fact when an instructor offers a specific example, especially one that follows something you have identified as a main point.

Other details worth recording in your notes are authorities. Authorities are experts, research studies, and other sources that lend weight to ideas and concepts. It is important not only to write down the ideas or issues that they bring to light, but also to note that this material comes from an authority and/or expert. Take the time to identify the authority in your notes.

You should also listen for opinions and facts and write them down in your notes. Facts are bits of information that are real or actual. Mainly they are provable, demonstrable pieces of information. In contrast, opinions are beliefs or conclusions held by someone that may not be objective or proven yet. It may be your opinion that facts are more important than opinions, but this is not necessarily so. An opinion on the future of nuclear physics that emanated from the mouth of the world's most prominent nuclear physicist, for example, would not be something to scoff at. What is important to you as a note-taker is to be sure you identify what is opinion and what is fact. Furthermore, although facts are supposed to be objective, there is little truly objective information in this world. Therefore, any time you question a fact or an opinion be sure to put a question mark in your notes, so you can follow up on it later.

Taking notes is not simply a matter of recording everything you hear. It is a process of absorbing information, assessing it, analyzing it, and then, finally, writing it down so that your notes reflect this process. To do this, begin to outline what you are hearing in your mind as you hear it, and before you write it down.

The speaking skills of your instructor will determine how hard you may need to work to understand what he or she has to say and then translate this into useful notes. Here are three strategies that instructors use to organize their lectures—you can use the strategies to help you organize your notes.

1. beginning—middle—end
2. relevant—irrelevant
3. theme—subtheme

Most lectures have a beginning, a middle, and an end. This is something you can listen for, and then structure your notes around. Try to divide what you hear, and also what you write down, into these three categories.

Some instructors tend to throw in irrelevant material during their lectures. Much of this does not belong in your notes and is a waste of time to write down. Learn to weed out irrelevant material. This is easier said than done because irrelevant material is not always easy to identify. For instance, some instructors use anecdotes to make important points. In these cases, you may have to listen for a few minutes to realize that an instructor is making an important point worth recording. A good strategy for taking notes is to take notes during class in a "draft" notebook. Then, after class, you can go through and reorganize, rewriting your notes into a "final" notebook.

Other instructors organize their lectures around themes and subthemes. If your instructor is organized, the difference between themes and subthemes will be obvious. If your instructor is disorganized, however, you will have to write all the themes down and then go back over them after the lecture to identify which points are main themes and which are subthemes.

Mapping Information

A map is a visual way of recording information that you hear or read. Indeed, you can map information about anything you are studying, whether you are in a classroom listening to a lecture or are sitting in the library reading a textbook. If you enjoy visualizing, this is a good study strategy for you because when you draw a map of information, the relationships between topics become clearly visible.

The good news is that you don't have to be an artist to draw an effective map because the process is quite straightforward. The first step is to get out a clean sheet of paper. Then, in the middle of that piece of paper, write down the main point, idea, or topic under consideration. Draw a circle around this main topic. Next, draw branches out from that center circle on which to record subtopics and details. Create as many branches as you need—or as many as will fit on your sheet of paper. On the top of the next page is an example of a simple map; it has only one level of subheadings.

The level of detail you include on each map depends on what you want to remember. Perhaps you already know one subject thoroughly but can't seem to remember any details about one or two particular subtopics. In that case, you can tailor the map to fit your needs. For example, consider a student who has studied all of the basic real estate principles covered in a typical real estate education course. He is very familiar with most of them. However, he

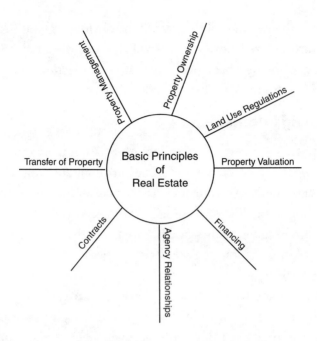

is having trouble with the subtopic of financing. This student should draw one or more maps in addition to the general map shown above. Each map should delve further into the topics and subtopics that he is having trouble with. On the top of the next page, you'll see examples of the types of map this student could draw.

Mapping information forces you to organize the information you are studying, whether that information is from your class notes, a special real estate lecture, or a real estate textbook. Sometimes, you will find that you need to spend considerable time to come up with an appropriate phrase, word, or sentence to write in the center circle of a map. Then you may need to spend even more time considering which topics are related to that main topic for the next level of branches. It is a process of making decisions

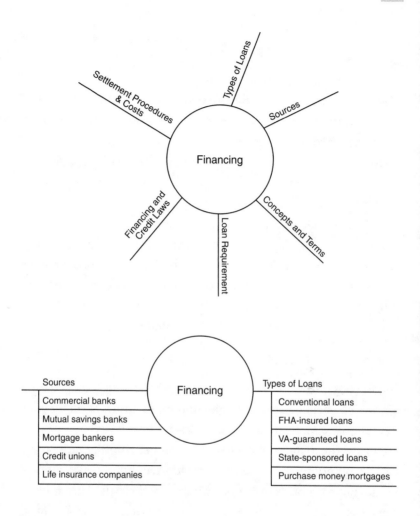

and connections between ideas and facts. That process alone makes drawing maps an effective study strategy. Another benefit is that after you complete a map, you have an excellent review aid. Because the material on a map is organized in a visual way, you will be able to recall that information more readily each time you review it. It gives the material you are studying a definite structure.

One way to use a map as a review aid is to take one out and study it carefully for five to ten minutes. Then, put it out of sight and attempt to redraw the entire map from memory. By forcing yourself to recall the items on the map, you ensure that those items are learned. You may find that you come up with additional information to add to the map while searching through your memory for the actual data you saw on the map.

Another way you can use a map you have created is to review it several days or weeks later. At that time, add more details to the map. You can look through a textbook or your notes to find additional information about the topic on your map, and pull out additional information to add to the map that you didn't include when you originally created the map.

Rewriting Notes

Taking the time to rewrite and reorganize the notes that you took in class can help you to remember important information for your real estate exam. Rewriting your notes not only gives you a chance to review the material, but also enables you to highlight the most important points. Because you have limited time to take notes in class, you may not always notice which points are the most important. But in a review of your notes, the important ideas and facts are more likely to surface because you have the advantage of having heard the material once before.

When you rewrite your notes, you are employing the strategy of repetition, which will help you to cement key concepts from your notes into your brain. By getting actively involved during your review of your notes by rewriting them, you log much more information into your memory than if you merely read through your notes.

Another benefit of rewriting your notes is that you can write them more legibly, since you will have more time to write in a study session than in class. This is especially helpful if you find that you are rushing in class to get your notes written and can't take the time to write carefully.

You can either rewrite your notes by hand, or you can take your handwritten notebook pages to a computer and type them up in an organized format. Just follow these eight steps:

1. While you are at the keyboard, take a few moments to think about your notes before you begin to type.
2. Come up with a title for the topic or topics your notes cover, and type this at the top of the page.
3. Continue to read through your notes, and each time you see an important point, type that point into the computer. It helps if you rewrite each point using different words because paraphrasing your own notes will help you to better understand and remember the material.
4. Add headings and subheadings to your notes to keep different topics separated.
5. Use **boldface** or ALL CAPS to emphasize key points.
6. Reorganize information from plain text into bullet points or numbered lists if possible. This can speed your review when you come back to look at your typed notes.

7. Print out the notes when you are finished and save them in a file, folder, or three-ring binder.

8. Review your typewritten notes regularly.

How to SCORE When Rewriting Your Notes!

Select	Select only the important information from your notes when you are in the process of rewriting them. Don't copy your notes verbatim.
Condense	Shorten long paragraphs or lists by writing a brief summary about the material.
Organize	Create headings and sub-headings, and rearrange the material in your notes to make it organized.
Rephrase	Use your own words as much as possible—especially if you tend to take notes without rephrasing the instructor's words.
Evaluate	As you rewrite your notes, take time to evaluate their effectiveness. If they seem lacking on a particular topic that was covered in class, ask a classmate if you can see his or her notes, too.

Creating Flash Cards

Designing flash cards to use as a study aid is a simple yet highly effective way to learn information. You can get creative when you sit down to make flash cards. For instance, you can use different-sized cards for different subjects, such as 4 × 6 cards for listing property and 3 × 5 cards for selling property. You can also use different colored index cards to organize your study material.

One advantage of creating flash cards is that you can carry them with you throughout the day because they fit easily into your backpack or purse—you may also want to cut 3 × 5 cards in half to get cards small enough to fit into your wallet or pocket. You can rotate the cards that you carry with you each day or week, so you can learn them all without having to carry a thick pile of cards every day. The number of flash cards you make is limited only by your time and inclination. You could conceivably create a flash card for every term listed in the glossary of this book.

Here are two sample flash cards:

Front of Card

Who can handle the details of a real estate closing?

Back of Card

■ an attorney ■ a real estate agent ■ a title company agent ■ an escrow company agent

Front of Card

What is earnest money?

Back of Card

an amount of money paid by a buyer as a deposit to indicate good faith intention to complete the transaction

Making Outlines

Creating outlines of the material you want to review can help you to organize that material in an orderly way. Plus, outlining gives you another tactic for studying and reviewing your real estate material. The outlining strategy is similar to the rewriting-your-notes strategy. The main difference is that outlines are more formal than notes. That is, there is a particular way outlines are organized. By organizing information the way they do, outlines help you remember ideas and information and see the relationships between those ideas. In an outline, you can see exactly how supporting information is related to main ideas.

The basic structure for an outline is this:

I. Topic
    A. Main Idea
        1. Major supporting idea
            a. Minor supporting idea

Outlines can have many layers and many variations, but this is essentially how they work: you start with the topic, move to the main idea, add the major supporting idea, and then list minor supporting ideas (if they seem important enough to write down). When you're working with a larger text, the overall main idea (topic) should be at the top. Here's an example of a partially completed outline:

I. Basic Principles of Real Estate
    A. Financing
        1. Types of loans

        a.   conventional loans

        b.   FHA-insured loans

        c.   VA-guaranteed loans

        d.   state-sponsored loans

        e.   purchase money mortgages

   2. Sources of loans

        a.   commercial banks

        b.   mutual savings banks

        c.   mortgage bankers

        d.   credit unions

        e.   life insurance companies

   3. Financing concepts and terms

   4. Loan repayment

   5. Financing and credit laws

   6. Settlement procedures and costs

B. Property Valuation

   1. Influences on property value

        a.   environmental

        b.   governmental/legal

        c.   life cycle

        d.   supply and demand

   2. Appraisal Process

        a.   market data approach

        b.   cost approach

        c.   income approach

   3. Legal considerations

   4. Appraisal standards and ethics

C. Land Use Regulations

D. Property Ownership

E. Agency Relationships

F. Transfer of Property
G. Contracts
H. Property Management

Outlining a text or your notes enables you to see the different layers of information and how they work together to support the overall main idea. Knowing and remembering the organization of facts can aid you greatly in your test preparation.

Using Highlighters

Another study strategy you can use to review important material for your upcoming real estate exam is to use highlighters and markers to mark up your textbook, test-preparation books, and notes. Marking the material you want to remember can help you to focus on the most important aspects and skip over the material you already know well or don't need to know for the exam. Highlighting words, phrases, and facts will help you to see and remember them while you review for your test.

The key to effective highlighting is to be selective. If you highlight every other word or sentence, you defeat your purpose. Too much will be highlighted and nothing will stand out.

So how do you know what's important enough to highlight? Part of it is simply to rely on your judgment. Which facts seem to matter most? Which facts are repeated in the text? Another way you can figure out the important facts in a text is to compare those facts with the questions asked on the practice tests you find in real estate test-preparation books. If you find that a topic is addressed on several practice tests, you can be sure that the topic warrants highlighting.

You may want to create an intricate system of using different colored highlighters for different topics. Or perhaps you want to use one color to highlight key terms and definitions and another color to highlight procedures or laws. Some people find that using too many colors is cumbersome, but others enjoy using a variety of colors.

Benefits of Highlighting

1. It requires you to make decisions about what is important.
2. It focuses your attention on important material.
3. It encourages you to spend more time with that material.
4. It improves your recall of the highlighted material.

Creating Audio Tapes

To help you learn and review important real estate information, you can use a recording device. Perhaps you want to read aloud unfamiliar information from a textbook and record it on a tape. Or, you could simply talk about the new information while the tape player records your observations and connections. The level of formality you use when talking into a tape player is up to you. Some people want to include asides and observations on their audiotapes, while others want to read aloud their texts word for word with no elaboration or extraneous comments. You could experiment with using tapes to remember several of the terms in the glossary of this book.

One of the advantages of using audiotapes for studying and reviewing material is that you can listen to the tapes throughout the day while you are driving in your car, going for a jog, or waiting in a dentist's office (if you have a portable tape player with earphones). Using the tapes throughout the day helps to solidify the material in your mind and gives you greater flexibility in your study schedule.

If you find that you really like to use audiotapes, you can set up a system of using different tapes for different topics. Then, you can color-code tape labels to keep the categories separate. Or you may want to listen to one tape, and then when you feel you know that material, you may want to record new material over it. However you decide to use audiotapes, remember to play back the tapes frequently since repetition is one of the best ways to learn complex information.

Making Connections

Connecting new material that you are learning to something that is already familiar to you will help you to better understand and remember the new material. Think of each connection as an individual string tying each item you want to learn to your brain. When you make several connections to a fact or idea, you create several strings to tie it down in your mind. Since one string can be easily broken, the more connections you make, the better. You want to create enough strings to the material to firmly anchor it in your memory.

For example, if you are studying occupancy terms and want to remember the particular situations in which a landlord is allowed to enter a tenant's property, you could try to make mental connections to each of the five situations:

1. in an emergency
2. to provide services or make repairs that were agreed to after giving reasonable notice to the tenant
3. to show property to prospective tenants after giving reasonable notice to the tenant
4. if the tenant has abandoned or surrendered the property
5. if a court orders or permits an entry

You may have rented an apartment sometime in the past. If so, try to recall an emergency incident that occurred while you were renting that apartment (maybe the landlord saved your pet cat from a fire). That would help you recall the first situation. Then, scan your mind for an example of a repair that a landlord had to make in your or a friend's rented home. Perhaps you will remember a time when a friend living in Florida needed her air conditioning unit fixed right away, so the landlord entered her apartment while she was at work.

Have you ever shown a rental property to a prospective tenant (situation 3)? Do you know of someone who moved suddenly and broke their lease by abandoning their apartment? And last, try to remember a specific friend, news report, or television show where a court order was obtained to enter a rental property.

The key to making strong connections is to concentrate on vivid mental pictures of a specific incidence that relates to each term or situation you want to recall. Spend a few minutes thinking about each item, so you can create a strong mental image—go ahead and fill in the details in your mind's eye. Try to involve your other senses as well—for example, by focusing on the smell of a particular abandoned building or the feel of how hot it was in the apartment with no air conditioning. Involve as many senses as possible to create truly memorable connections.

You may find that this study strategy works well when you use it to study and recall main ideas, rather than smaller details about a topic. That's because the more detailed the information you want to recall, the less likely you are to know of a specific case you can connect it to in your own experience. In the example above, you can see how creating mental images of past events with which you are familiar could help you to remember the five situations in which a landlord is allowed to enter a tenant's property. However, to recall more detailed information about the tenant's right of possession of the property and the tenant's quiet enjoyment of the leased property, you may want to use another study strategy.

The last study strategy covered in this book is the use of mnemonics (also known as memory tricks). It is such an important and distinct study strategy that there is a chapter devoted just to mnemonics.

Chapter 3

Mnemonics

Mnemonics are memory tricks that can help you to remember important pieces of information. This chapter shows how you can create and use different mnemonics to help you remember essential real estate information for your upcoming exam.

Two popular mnemonic devices, which you may have already used at some time in your previous academic studies, are *acronyms* and *acrostics*. Two additional mnemonic devices that are not quite as well known as acronyms and acrostics—but can be just as useful—are the *place* and *peg* methods.

The best time to create mnemonics is after you've spent considerable time studying a particular real estate topic. That's because mnemonics help you *recall* information with which you are already familiar—they don't help you to understand *new* material. Now, let's take a closer look at some mnemonics you can use.

CREATING ACRONYMS

The most common type of mnemonic is the *acronym*. An acronym is a word created from the first letters in a series of words. One acronym you may already know is HOMES, which is a word created by using the first letter from each of the names of the Great Lakes:

Huron
Ontario
Michigan
Erie
Superior

You could also make up a silly word to help you remember a list of terms. A common acronym that helps students to remember the colors of the visible spectrum is the nonsense word "roygbiv." You could also write the word as a person's name if that helps you to remember the letters: "Roy G. Biv."

Red
Orange
Yellow
Green
Blue
Indigo
Violet

You can create an acronym for just about anything you want to remember. Therefore, you can use acronyms to help you remember the material you are studying for a real estate exam.

Even though it will take you a few minutes to create an acronym, that extra time can pay off during your exam when you are able to recall important information. There is no limit to how many acronyms you can create. It's up to you to decide how much time you want to spend creating and memorizing acronyms to help you store and recall the real estate material you need to know on exam day. To begin, just try to create one acronym. See how long it takes you and how comfortable you are with the process. You may then want to try using some of the other mnemonics too, so you can get a sense of which ones work best for you.

Follow these steps to create your own acronyms:

1. Decide on a particular list of terms you want to memorize or a certain number of steps in a real estate transaction you want to be able to recall.
2. Write down those terms or steps on a sheet of paper.
3. Take a close look at the letters that begin each word or phrase. If one or more phrases in your list begin with the same word, you may need to consider substituting another word that means the same thing or rearranging the words in a phrase.
4. If the order of the words, phrases, or steps is not essential, you can rearrange them.
5. Get creative and brainstorm to find one or more words that consist of the first letters of the main terms or phrases in your original list.
6. Pick the acronym from your brainstorming list that you are most likely to remember based on your own experience, memory, and knowledge.

7. Arrange the terms or phrases you want to recall in the order of your chosen acronym. Use highlighting or boldface to set off the first letter of each term or phrase so when you review, it will be easier to see the acronym.

Here is an example of how one student used these seven steps to create an acronym.

1. I want to memorize some of the different types of commercial properties.
2. Apartment buildings, hotels and motels, office buildings, retail buildings, and storage facilities.
3. I'm going to change the order of the words *motels* and *hotels*.
4. The order of terms is not essential, so I can rearrange them as follows: retail buildings, office buildings, apartment buildings, motels and hotels, and storage facilities.
5. ROAMS and M. SOAR are the only two words I can think of for this list of terms.
6. I think it will be easier to remember the word ROAMS because it is just one word. I can think of a person going to all the different types of commercial properties as 'roaming' from one type of property to another.
7. Some of the different types of commercial property are:
   Retail buildings
   Office buildings

Apartment buildings
Motels and hotels
Storage facilities

Here are a few more examples of acronyms that are specifically related to real estate information:

1. To help you remember the elements that establish value for a property's appraisal, you can think of the word DUST, which stands for:
   Demand for the type of property
   Utility (desirable use) the property offers
   Scarcity of properties available
   Transferability of the property to a new owner (lack of impediments to a sale)

2. To remember the five steps that courts use to determine whether an item is a fixture and thus part of the real property, you can use the name MARIA:
   Method of attachment
   Agreement of the parties, which can override all other considerations
   Relationship of the parties—in a residential sale or lease, legislatures and courts tend to favor the buyer/tenant
   Intention of the party who attached the item to the land or building
   Adaptability of the item for another use or location

Sometimes it helps to use humor when creating acronyms, because if something amuses you, it will be easier to remember. For example, you can imagine a Martian (who happens to live for free on Mars) coming to earth and being shocked by the fact that we have to include so many things in our monthly housing payment. This Martian *pities* us earthlings. Creating a short scenario like this can help you recall the word PITI, which stands for the four main categories that make up a homeowner's monthly payment for housing.

Principal
Interest
Taxes on the property
Insurance

Once you invest the time to create some acronyms, review them on a consistent basis. You can rewrite them or read them aloud during your scheduled study sessions. You can also reread them whenever you find a free moment during your day. The key to memorizing mnemonics is repetition, so study your acronyms over and over until they become familiar friends.

CREATING ACROSTICS

Another type of mnemonic is a silly sentence or phrase, known as an *acrostic*, which is made out of words that each begin with the letter or letters that start each item in a series that you want to remember. For example, *Please Excuse My Dear Aunt Sally* is a silly sentence that math students often use to help them remember the order of operations:

Please **E**xcuse **M**y **D**ear **A**unt **S**ally

Parentheses
Exponents
Multiply

Divide
Add
Subtract

Here's another example of an acrostic. To recall the letters of the notes on the lines of the treble clef (E, G, B, D, and F), music students often recite this acrostic:

Every **G**ood **B**oy **D**oes **F**ine

If you know the first letter of a word you cannot recall, your chances of recalling that word are much higher than if you did not know the first letter of it. Therefore, using an acrostic can help you to recall a forgotten word after a few moments of thinking about the letter that word starts with. This can help you to overcome memory block during a real estate exam.

The steps for creating acrostics are similar to the steps for creating acronyms. The steps are shown below:

1. Decide which terms, phrases, or steps you want to memorize.
2. Write down those items on a sheet of paper.
3. Take a close look at the letters that begin each word or phrase on your paper. Spend a few minutes thinking about those letters.
4. If the order of the terms is not essential, try rearranging the items in a few different ways.
5. Spend time brainstorming to create a phrase or silly sentence in which each word begins with the same letter of the terms in your original list.

6. Pick the acrostic that you are most likely to remember based on your own experience, memory, and knowledge.

7. Arrange the terms you want to recall in the order of your chosen acrostic. Highlight the first letter of each term, so when you review it will be easier to recall the acrostic.

Here is an example of how a student created an acrostic by using the seven steps above:

1. I want to memorize the four ways a real estate contract can be terminated.

2. Completion of the terms of the contract, mutual consent of the parties (rescission), breach by one of the parties, or destruction of the property

3. C, M or R, B, D

4. The order of terms is not essential.

5. Here is my brainstorming list of acrostics: Can monkeys be dumb? Real boys don't cry. My dog can bark.

6. I chose the acrostic "My dog can bark" because I like the visual and auditory clues it gives me. Thinking about my dog barking is easy to link to terminating a contract because both occurrences sometimes have unpleasant connotations.

7. The four ways a real estate contract can be terminated:

My Dog Can Bark

Mutual consent of the parties (rescission)
Destruction of the property
Completion of the terms of the contract
Breach by one of the parties

When creating an acrostic, remember that you will have an easier time memorizing a phrase or sentence that you can identify with, are interested in, or find humorous. So when you get to step six, take the time you need to come up with an interesting phrase or sentence. For instance, if you love to eat sweets, you might want to use words associated with foods when creating an acrostic. Here is an example of an acrostic to help a student remember the ways a purchase offer from a buyer to a seller can be terminated:

Rich Chocolate Rules

Revocation of the buyer before the seller's acceptance
Counteroffer given by the seller
Rejection by the seller

Whatever theme you decide to use, don't be afraid to branch out and try others. Making up acrostics is a creative process, so once you get started, you may find it hard to stop! Once you have created some acrostics, you will need to review them several times before exam day to make sure they are firmly lodged in your memory. You may want to rewrite them over and over again (using repetition to help you memorize them). Or you may want to read them aloud during your scheduled study sessions. You can also write them on index cards and carry them with you to read throughout the day. Remember, the best way to memorize mnemonics is through repetition, so spend time reviewing your acrostics until you know them backward and forward.

ORGANIZING ACRONYMS AND ACROSTICS

Since you will have many terms and definitions to remember for your real estate exam, consider creating a system to help you organize the acronyms and acrostics that you plan to use during your study sessions. A good way to do this is to put the terms you want to memorize into categories by subject. For instance, put together all the terms relating to property management in one group, and all those relating to financing in another. This will help you keep track of the mnemonics that you've created.

You can go a step further in organizing your acronyms and acrostics by using a color-coding system. Use different colored sheets of paper or index cards to create your system. Use a different color for each subject. For example, you can write out all the mnemonics you've developed for property management topics on blue pieces of paper and all those for financing on green ones. When you casually glance at your paper, you will know immediately which mnemonics are related by subject just by noticing the color of the paper the mnemonic is written on.

Keep in mind that each person's subject categories may be somewhat different; that's okay. One person may put the Federal Fair Housing Laws under the subject of property management and another person may put it under the subject of working with buyers. The exact placement of an item in a subject category is not as important as your knowledge of the relationship of that item to other items in its category. Going through the process of selecting subject categories for your acronyms and acrostics is a good way to get an overview of your real estate study material.

Your list of specific items to remember in each subject category will likely differ from another person's because everyone comes to the real estate material with a unique background. Perhaps you already know several of the terms in one subject, but have a hard time recalling terms in another subject. Some people entering the real estate profession have previous sales or finance experience in which they have already become familiar with several relevant concepts and terms. So each person studying for a real estate exam can focus on the subject categories in which he or she needs the most practice. The more terms you need to learn, the more acronyms and acrostics you may want to use.

If you decide to use a color-coding system to organize your acronyms and acrostics, then be sure to keep several sheets of colored paper or index cards on hand, so you will have an ample supply that will last throughout your entire study plan. You don't want to run out of blue paper just when you come up with a truly terrific acronym or acrostic for those few extra property management terms you didn't notice at the beginning of your study schedule. Once you develop a color-coding system, stick to it so that you don't get confused about which terms go with each color.

One of the benefits of using a color-coding system is that even if you forget one of the acronyms or acrostics you create, you may still be able to see in your mind's eye the color of the paper it was written on. This visualization could help you at least recall the subject that a term is related to. Believe it or not, you could get an extra point or two on exam day just from this knowledge. Here's an example:

What does the term "comps" refer to?
   a.   executed contracts
   b.   recent nearby sales
   c.   addendums
   d.   closing costs

Let's say that after you read the question and all the possible answers, you still have no recollection of what the term "*comps*" means. A great thing about using a color-coding system to keep your mnemonics organized into separate categories is that it can help you to recall the subject a term is related to. So, even though you don't remember the definition of *comps*, you do recall that the term was a part of a mnemonic that was written on yellow paper. You know that all the mnemonics you wrote on yellow paper are related to the appraisal process—and none of the other answer choices are related to the appraisal process. Therefore, you can confidently pick **b** as the correct answer through the process of elimination. The term "comps" refers to the recent nearby sales of comparable properties, whose prices are analyzed in the market sales approach to appraisal.

One of the best ways to memorize acronyms and acrostics is through the use of repetition and your own specific learning style. For kinesthetic or tactile learners, those who learn by touching or doing, writing out each mnemonic several times will help to seal it in your memory. Auditory learners, those who learn best by listening, might remember the information better if they repeat the acronym or acrostic out loud, over and over. Visual learners, those who learn best by looking, might need to look only at the acronym or acrostic until it is fixed in their mind.

USING THE PLACE METHOD

One of the oldest mnemonics that is still in use today is called the method of *loci*; it was first recorded over 2,500 years ago. Today it is often called the *place method*. The first step in using the place method is to think about a place you know very well: perhaps your living room or bedroom. You need to think of a place that has several items (pieces of furniture or other large items) that always remain in the same place. These items become your landmarks or anchors in the place method mnemonic. You need to remember where each landmark is in the room and when you visualize walking around this room, you must always walk in the same direction (an easy way to be consistent is to always move around the room in a clockwise direction). Then the next step is to assign an item that you want to memorize to each landmark in your room. A good way to do this is to actually see each word attached to each landmark. Here's an example of how one student used the place method to remember the different ways a listing agreement can be terminated. This example uses landmarks in the student's bedroom.

Place Method Sample

Landmark		Ways a Listing Agreement Can Be Terminated
1. Doorway of room	→	**1.** Performance—a successful transaction or other fulfillment by the agent of the terms of the agreement
2. Two small chairs	→	**2.** Mutual consent of the parties
3. TV stand	→	**3.** Revocation by the property owner, who may be liable for damages to the agent
4. Large vase with flowers	→	**4.** Death or adjudicated incompetency of either owner or agent
5. Nightstand w/table lamp	→	**5.** Expiration of the time period specified in the agreement
6. Bed	→	**6.** Abandonment (inaction) by the agent
7. Closet	→	**7.** Destruction of the property

In this example, the student imagines each way of terminating a listing agreement as being separate from the others and relates each one to a different landmark in her room. For example, as she steps through the doorway of her bedroom, she imagines a listing agreement that was successfully fulfilled by the agent. Then she sees the two small chairs just inside the doorway and imagines each party of the agreement sitting in a chair, mutually agreeing to terminate the agreement. She visualizes the property owner revoking his side of the agreement on the television that sits on the TV stand, and she imagines that the large vase of flowers next to the TV stand is at the funeral of the property owner. As she thinks about the next item in her room, she imagines turning off the table lamp on her nightstand and the room becoming dark—this is linked to the expiration of the time period specified in the agreement. In this way, she continues to visually link each item in her room to one of the ways a listing agreement may be terminated.

To make the place method work, you must first study and understand each term, phrase, or step you want to remember, so you can visualize each item and directly link it to each landmark in your chosen place. The more vivid your visualization is, the stronger the connection will be between the items you want to recall and the landmarks that are already entrenched in your memory.

As you can imagine, it takes some time to create the connections from the landmarks in your special place to the items you want to remember, but that time will be well spent if it helps you achieve a higher score on your real estate exam. The amount

You can USE the Place Method

Understand the information you want to memorize.
Select the landmarks you want to attach the information to.
Encode the landmarks by attaching the information you want to memorize.

of time you spend on creating mnemonics using the place method is up to you—you can spend many hours creating several elaborate place method scenarios, or you can spend a few minutes devising just one.

If you've never heard of the place method before, you may want to start asking waiters and waitresses who don't write down their customers' orders how they remember who gets what. You may find that they use the place method to keep track of people's orders because it works so well.

USING THE PEG METHOD

Another mnemonic that can help you recall information for your upcoming real estate exam is called the *peg method*. The peg method is similar to the place method, but it uses numbers and a rhyme instead of landmarks in a location as a way to remember important information. In essence, you use each line in the rhyme as a familiar "peg" on which to hang each item that you want to remember. An advantage the peg method has over the place method is that you can recall items in any order instead of having to go through the entire sequence to recall one of the items in the middle of the list.

The first step in using the peg method is to memorize the simple rhyme that appears below. You will need to know this rhyme by heart, so you can use the numbers in it as the landmarks for linking the new information to. Here is the rhyme:

> One is a bun
> Two is a shoe
> Three is a tree

Four is a door
Five is a hive
Six is sticks
Seven is heaven
Eight is a gate
Nine is wine
Ten is a hen

Remember, to make the peg method work, you must commit this rhyme to memory. Once you memorize the rhyme, you can use it any time you need to remember things, not just for recalling information for a real estate exam. After you memorize the rhyme, the next step is to compile a list of terms you want to remember. Then, simply picture the first new term you want to learn with the first word in the rhyme (bun). Then picture the second word you want to learn with the second word in the rhyme (shoe). Here's an example of how one student used the peg method to recall the different forms of concurrent ownership.

Peg Method Sample

Word in Rhyme		Form of Concurrent Ownership
1. bun	→	1. joint tenancy
2. shoe	→	2. tenancy in common
3. tree	→	3. tenancy by the entirety
4. door	→	4. tenancy in partnership
5. hive	→	5. community property
6. sticks	→	6. joint venture
7. heaven	→	7. corporation
8. gate	→	8. limited liability company

9. wine   →   **9.** syndicate
10. hen   →   **10.** trust

In this example, a student creates visual images that link each word in the rhyme to a different form of concurrent ownership. The student has already studied the forms of concurrent ownership, so he knows what the different forms mean. To begin creating visual links, the student imagines a married couple who own their home as joint tenants. He then visualizes the wife eating a hot cross *bun* at the funeral of her husband. The wife enjoys her hot cross bun because she has the right of survivorship, which is featured in the joint tenancy form of concurrent ownership.

Then, for the second item, he imagines two sisters who own their home as tenants in common. He visualizes one of the sisters as having a rock in her *shoe* at the funeral of the other sister. The rock makes the sister uncomfortable—she is uncomfortable because she does not have the right of survivorship and is worried about what will happen to her sister's share of the house. The student then creates similar mental images for each additional item on the list.

If you want to use the peg method and make it work for you, you must first study and understand each item you want to remember, so you can visualize an example of each item and directly link it to each word in the rhyme. The more vivid your visualizations are, the stronger the connections will be between the items you want to recall and the words in the rhyme that you've already memorized.

Learning and using the mnemonic devices in this chapter can help you achieve a top score on your upcoming real estate exam. Before you know it, you will be a real estate expert. Just continue your solid studying habits throughout your real estate career, and you will be able to successfully meet each new challenge that arises.

Chapter 4

Real Estate Glossary

HOW TO USE THE GLOSSARY

This glossary contains over 500 terms that will help you not only as you study for your healthcare exam, but also after you pass your exam and are practicing in the field. The terms are listed in alphabetical order for easy reference.

A

abstract of title   a certified summary of the history of a title to a particular parcel of real estate that includes the original grant and all subsequent transfers, encumbrances, and releases.

acceleration clause   a clause in a note, mortgage, or deed of trust that permits the lender to declare the entire amount of principal and accrued interest due and payable immediately in the event of default.

acceptance   the indication by a party receiving an offer that they agree to the terms of the offer. In most states the offer and acceptance must be reduced to writing when real property is involved.

accretion   the increase or addition of land resulting from the natural deposit of sand or soil by streams, lakes, or rivers.

accrued depreciation   (1) the amount of depreciation, or loss in value, that has accumulated since initial construction; (2) the difference between the current appraised value and the cost to replace the building new.

accrued items   a list of items of expenses that have been incurred but have not yet been paid, such as interest on a mortgage loan, that are included on a closing statement.

acre   a measure of land equal to 43,560 square feet or 4,840 square yards.

actual eviction   the result of legal action brought by a landlord against a defaulted tenant, whereby the tenant is physically removed from rented or leased property by a court order.

actual notice   the actual knowledge that a person has of a particular fact.

addendum   any provision added to a contract, or an addition to a contract that expands, modifies, or enhances the clarity of the agreement. To be a part of the contract and legally enforceable, an addendum must be referenced within the contract.

adjacent   lying near to but not necessarily in actual contact with.

adjoining   contiguous or attached; in actual contact with.

adjustable-rate mortgage (ARM)   a mortgage in which the interest changes periodically, according to corresponding fluctuations in an index. All ARMs are tied to indexes. For example, a seven-year, adjustable-rate mortgage is a loan where the rate remains fixed for the first seven years, then fluctuates according to the index to which it is tied.

adjusted basis   the original cost of a property, plus acquisition costs, plus the value of added improvements to the property, minus accrued depreciation.

adjustment date   the date the interest rate changes on an adjustable-rate mortgage.

ad valorem tax   tax in proportion to the value of a property.

adverse possession   a method of acquiring title to another person's property through court action after taking actual, open, hostile, and continuous possession for a statutory period of time; may require payment of property taxes during the period of possession.

affidavit   a written statement made under oath and signed before a licensed public official, usually a notary public.

agency   the legal relationship between principal and agent that arises out of a contract wherein an agent is employed to do certain acts on behalf of the principal who has retained the agent to deal with a third party.

agent   one who has been granted the authority to act on behalf of another.

alienation   the transfer of ownership of a property to another, either voluntarily or involuntarily.

alienation clause   the clause in a mortgage or deed of trust that permits the lender to declare all unpaid principal and accrued interest due and payable if the borrower transfers title to the property.

allodial system   in the United States, a system of land ownership in which land is held free and clear of any rent or services due to the government; commonly contrasted with the feudal system, in which ownership is held by a monarch.

amenities   features or benefits of a particular property that enhance the property's desirability and value, such as a scenic view or a pool.

amortization   the method of repaying a loan or debt by making periodic installment payments composed of both principal and interest. When all principal has been repaid, it is considered fully amortized.

amortization schedule   a table that shows how much of each loan payment will be applied toward principal and how much toward interest over the lifespan of the loan. It also shows the gradual decrease of the outstanding loan balance until it reaches zero.

amortize   to repay a loan through regular payments that are comprised of principal and interest.

annual percentage rate (APR)   the total or effective amount of interest charged on a loan, expressed as a percentage, on a yearly basis. This value is created according to a government formula intended to reflect the true annual cost of borrowing.

anti-deficiency law   laws used in some states to limit the claim of a lender on default on payment of a purchase money mortgage on owner-occupied residential property to the value of the collateral.

anti-trust laws laws designed to protect free enterprise and the open marketplace by prohibiting certain business practices that restrict competition. In reference to real estate, these laws would prevent such practices as price-fixing or agreements by brokers to limit their areas of trade.

apportionments adjustment of income, expenses, or carrying charges related to of real estate, usually computed to the date of closing so that the seller pays all expenses to date, then the buyer pays all expenses beginning on the closing date.

appraisal an estimate or opinion of the value of an adequately described property, as of a specific date.

appraised value an opinion of a property's fair market value, based on an appraiser's knowledge, experience, and analysis of the property, based on comparable sales.

appraiser an individual qualified by education, training, and experience to estimate the value of real property. Appraisers may work directly for mortgage lenders, or they may be independent contractors.

appreciation an increase in the market value of a property.

appurtenance something that transfers with the title to land even if not an actual part of the property, such as an easement.

arbitration the process of settling a dispute in which the parties submit their differences to an impartial third party, on whose decision on the matter is binding.

assessed value   the value of a property used to calculate real estate taxes.

assessor   a public official who establishes the value of a property for taxation purposes.

assessment   the process of assigning value on property for taxation purposes.

asset   items of value owned by an individual. Assets that can be quickly converted into cash are considered "liquid assets," such as bank accounts and stock portfolios. Other assets include real estate, personal property, and debts owed.

assignment   the transfer of rights or interest from one person to another.

assumption of mortgage   the act of acquiring the title to a property that has an existing mortgage and agreeing to be liable for the payment of any debt still existing on that mortgage. However, the lender must accept the transfer of liability for the original borrower to be relieved of the debt.

attachment   the process whereby a court takes custody of a debtor's property until the creditor's debt is satisfied.

attest   to bear witness by providing a signature.

attorney-in-fact   a person who is authorized under a power of attorney to act on behalf of another.

avulsion   the removal of land from one owner to another when a stream or other body of water suddenly changes its channel.

B

balloon mortgage   a loan in which the periodic payments do not fully amortize the loan, so that a final payment (a balloon payment) substantially larger than the amount of the periodic payments must be made to satisfy the debt.

balloon payment   the final, lump-sum payment that is due at the termination of a balloon mortgage.

bankruptcy   an individual or individuals can restructure or relieve themselves of debts and liabilities by filing in federal bankruptcy court. There are many types of bankruptcies, and the most common for an individual is "Chapter 7 No Asset," which relieves the borrower of most types of debts.

base line   one of the imaginary east-west lines used as a reference point when describing property with the rectangular or government survey method of property description.

beneficiary   (1) one who benefits from the acts of another; (2) the lender in a deed of trust.

bequest   personal property given by provision of a will.

betterment   an improvement to property that increases its value.

bill of sale   a written instrument that transfers ownership of personal property. A bill of sale cannot be used to transfer ownership of real property, which is passed by deed.

binder   an agreement, accompanied by an earnest money deposit for the purchase of a piece of real estate, to show the purchaser's good faith intent to complete a transaction.

biweekly mortgage   a mortgage in which payments are made every two weeks instead of once a month. Therefore, instead of making twelve monthly payments during the year, the borrower makes the equivalent of thirteen monthly payments. The extra payment reduces the principal, thereby reducing the time it takes to pay off a thirty-year mortgage.

blanket mortgage   a mortgage in which more than one parcel of real estate is pledged to cover a single debt.

bona fide   in good faith, honest.

bond   evidence of personal debt secured by a mortgage or other lien on real estate.

boot   money or property provided to make up a difference in value or equity between two properties in an exchange.

branch office   a place of business secondary to a principal office. The branch office is a satellite office generally run by a licensed broker, for the benefit of the broker running the principal office, as well as the associate broker's convenience.

breach of contract   violation of any conditions or terms in a contract without legal excuse.

broker   the term "broker" can mean many things, but in terms of real estate, it is the owner-manager of a business that brings together the parties to a real estate transaction for a fee. The roles of brokers and brokers' associates are defined by state law. In the mortgage industry, broker usually refers to a company or individual that does not lend the money for the loans directly, but brokers loans to larger lenders or investors.

brokerage   the business of bringing together buyers and sellers or other participants in a real estate transaction.

broken opinion (BPO)   a broker's opinion of value based on a comparative market analysis, rather than a certified appraisal.

building code   local regulations that control construction, design, and materials used in construction that are based on health and safety regulations.

building line   the distance from the front, rear, or sides of a building lot beyond which no structures may extend.

buydown   usually refers to a fixed-rate mortgage where the interest rate is "bought down" for a temporary period, usually one to three years. After that time and for the remainder of the term, the borrower's payment is calculated at the note rate. In order to buy down the initial rate for the temporary payment, a lump sum is paid and held in an account used to supplement the borrower's monthly payment. These funds usually come from the seller as a financial incentive to induce someone to buy their property.

buyer's broker   real estate broker retained by a prospective buyer; this buyer becomes the broker's client to whom fiduciary duties are owed.

bylaws   rules and regulations adopted by an association—for example, a condominium.

C

cancellation clause   a provision in a lease that confers on one or all parties to the lease the right to terminate the parties' obligations, should the occurrence of the condition or contingency set forth in the clause happen.

canvassing   the practice of searching for prospective clients by making unsolicited phone calls and/or visiting homes door-to-door.

cap   the limit on fluctuation rates regarding adjustable rate mortgages. Limitations, or caps may apply to how much the loan may adjust over a six-month period, an annual period, and over the life of the loan. There is also a limit on how much that payment can change each year.

capital   money used to create income, or the net worth of a business as represented by the amount by which its assets exceed its liabilities.

capital expenditure   the cost of a betterment to a property.

capital gains tax   a tax charged on the profit gained from the sale of a capital asset.

capitalization   the process of estimating the present value of an income-producing piece of property by dividing anticipated future income by a capitalization rate.

capitalization rate   the rate of return a property will generate on an owner's investment.

cash flow   the net income produced by an investment property, calculated by deducting operating and fixed expenses from gross income.

caveat emptor   let the buyer beware [*Latin*].

CC&R covenants, conditions, and restrictions of a cooperative or condominium development.

certificate of discharge a document used when the security instrument is a mortgage.

certificate of eligibility a document issued by the Veterans Administration that certifies a veteran's eligibility for a VA loan.

certificate of reasonable value (CRV) once the appraisal has been performed on a property being bought with a VA loan, the Veterans Administration issues a CRV.

certificate of sale the document given to a purchaser of real estate that is sold at a tax foreclosure sale.

certificate of title a report stating an opinion on the status of a title, based on the examination of public records.

chain of title the recorded history of conveyances and encumbrances that affect the title to a parcel of land.

city a large municipality governed under a charter and granted by the state.

clear title a title that is free of liens and legal questions as to ownership of a property that is a requirement for the sale of real estate; sometimes referred to as just title, good title, or free and clear.

closing the point in a real estate transaction when the purchase price is paid to the seller and the deed to the property is transferred from the seller to the buyer.

closing costs there are two kinds: (1) "non-recurring closing costs" and (2) "pre-paid items." "Non-recurring closing costs" are any items paid once as a result of buying the property or obtaining a loan. "Pre-paid items" are items that recur over time, such as property taxes and homeowners insurance. A lender makes an attempt to estimate the amount of non-recurring closing costs and pre-paid items on the good faith estimate, which is issued to the borrower within three days of receiving a home loan application.

closing date   the date on which the buyer takes over the property.

closing statement   a written accounting of funds received and disbursed during a real estate transaction. Buyer and seller receive separate closing statements.

cloud on the title   an outstanding claim or encumbrance that can affect or impair the owner's title.

clustering   the grouping of home sites within a subdivision on smaller lots than normal, with the remaining land slated for use as common areas.

codicil   a supplement or addition to a will that modifies the original instrument.

coinsurance clause   a clause in an insurance policy that requires the insured to pay a portion of any loss experienced.

collateral   something of value hypothecated (real property) or pledged (personal property) by a borrower as security for a debt.

collection   when a borrower falls behind, the lender contacts the borrower in an effort to bring the loan current. The loan goes to "collection."

color of title   an instrument that gives evidence of title, but may not be legally adequate to actually convey title.

commission   the fee paid to a broker for services rendered in a real estate transaction.

commitment letter   a pledge in writing affirming an agreement.

common law   the body of law derived from local custom and judicial precedent.

common areas   portions of a building, land, and amenities owned (or managed) by a planned unit development or condominium project's homeowners' association or a cooperative project's cooperative corporation. These areas are used by all of the unit owners, who share in the common expenses of their operation and maintenance. Common areas may include swimming pools, tennis courts, and other recreational facilities, as well as common corridors of buildings, parking areas, and lobbies.

community property   a system of property ownership in which each spouse has equal interest in property acquired during the marriage; recognized in nine states.

comparable sales   recent sales of similar properties in nearby areas that are used to help estimate the current market value of a property.

competent parties   people who are legally qualified to enter a contract, usually meaning that they are of legal age, of sound mind, and not under the influence of drugs or other mind-altering substances.

competitive market analysis (CMA)   an analysis intended to assist a seller or buyer in determining a property's range of value.

condominium   a form of ownership in which an individual owns a specific unit in a multi-unit building and shares ownership of common areas with other unit owners.

condominium conversion   changing the ownership of an existing building (usually a multi-dwelling rental unit) from single ownership to condominium ownership.

consideration   something of value that induces parties to enter into a contract, such as money or services.

construction mortgage   a short-term loan used to finance the building of improvements to real estate.

constructive eviction   action or inaction by a landlord that renders a property uninhabitable, forcing a tenant to move out with no further liability for rent.

constructive notice   notice of a fact given by making the fact part of the public record. All persons are responsible for knowing the information, whether or not they have actually seen the record.

contingency   a condition that must be met before a contract is legally binding. A satisfactory home inspection report from a qualified home inspector is an example of a common type of contingency.

contract   an agreement between two or more legally competent parties to do or to refrain from doing some legal act in exchange for a consideration.

contract for deed   a contract for the sale of a parcel of real estate in which the buyer makes periodic payments to the seller and receives title to the property only after all, or a substantial part, of the purchase price has been paid, or regular payments have been made for one year or longer.

conventional loan   a loan that is neither insured or guaranteed by an agency of government.

conversion option   an option in an adjustable-rate mortgage to convert it to a fixed-rate mortgage.

convertible ARM   an adjustable-rate mortgage that allows the borrower to change the ARM to a fixed-rate mortgage at a specific time.

conveyance   the transfer of title from the grantor to the grantee.

cooperative   a form of property ownership in which a corporation owns a multi-unit building and stockholders of the corporation may lease and occupy individual units of the building through a proprietary lease.

corporation   a legal entity with potentially perpetual existence that is created and owned by shareholders who appoint a board of directors to direct the business affairs of the corporation.

counteroffer   an offer submitted in response to an offer. It has the effect of overriding the original offer.

credit   an agreement in which a borrower receives something of value in exchange for a promise to repay the lender.

credit history   a record of an individual's repayment of debt.

cul-de-sac   a dead-end street that widens at the end, creating a circular turnaround area.

courtesy   the statutory or common law right of a husband to all or part of real estate owned by his deceased wife, regardless of will provisions not recognized in community property states.

curtilage   area of land occupied by a building, its outbuildings, and yard, either actually enclosed or considered enclosed.

D

damages   the amount of money recoverable by a person who has been injured by the actions of another.

datum   a specific point used in surveying.

DBA   the abbreviation for "doing business as."

debt   an amount owed to another.

decedent   a person who dies.

deed   a written document that, when properly signed and delivered, conveys title to real property from the grantor to the grantee.

deed-in-lieu   a foreclosure instrument used to convey title to the lender when the borrower is in default and wants to avoid foreclosure.

deed of trust   a deed in which the title to property is transferred to a third party trustee to secure repayment of a loan; three-party mortgage arrangement.

deed restriction   an imposed restriction for the purpose of limiting the use of land, such as the size or type of improvements to be allowed. Also called a restrictive covenant.

default   the failure to perform a contractual duty.

defeasance clause   a clause in a mortgage that renders it void where all obligations have been fulfilled.

deficiency judgment   a personal claim against a borrower when mortgaged property is foreclosed and sale of the property does not produce sufficient funds to pay off the mortgage. Deficiency judgments may be prohibited in some circumstances by anti-deficiency protection.

delinquency   failure to make mortgage or loan payments when payments are due.

depreciation   a loss in value due to physical deterioration, functional, or external obsolescence.

descent   the transfer of property to an owner's heirs when the owner dies intestate.

devise   the transfer of title to real estate by will.

devisee   one who receives a bequest of real estate by will.

devisor   one who grants real estate by will.

directional growth   the direction toward which certain residential sections of a city are expected to grow.

discount point   one percent of the loan amount charged by a lender at closing to increase a loan's effective yield and lower the fare rate to the borrower.

discount rate   the rate that lenders pay for mortgage funds—a higher rate is passed on to the borrower.

dispossess   to remove a tenant from property by legal process.

dominant estate (tenement)   property that includes the right to use an easement on adjoining property.

dower   the right of a widow in the property of her husband upon his death in noncommunity property states.

down payment   the part of the purchase price that the buyer pays in cash and is not financed with a mortgage or loan.

dual agency   an agent who represents both parties in a transaction.

due-on-sale clause   a provision in a mortgage that allows the lender to demand repayment in full if the borrower sells the property that serves as security for the mortgage.

duress   the use of unlawful means to force a person to act or to refrain from an action against his or her will.

E

earnest money   down payment made by a buyer of real estate as evidence of good faith.

easement   the right of one party to use the land of another for a particular purpose, such as to lay utility lines.

easement by necessity   an easement, granted by law and requiring court action that is deemed necessary for the full enjoyment of a parcel of land. An example would be an easement allowing access from land-locked property to a road.

easement by prescription   a means of acquiring an easement by continued, open, and hostile use of someone else's property for a statuatorily defined period of time.

easement in gross   a personal right granted by an owner with no requirement that the easement holder own adjoining land.

economic life   the period of time over which an improved property will generate sufficient income to justify its continued existence.

effective age   an appraiser's estimate of the physical condition of a building. The actual age of a building may be different than its effective age.

emblements   cultivated crops; generally considered to be personal property.

eminent domain   the right of a government to take private property for public use upon payment of its fair market value. Eminent domain is the basis for condemnation proceedings.

encroachment   a trespass caused when a structure, such as a wall or fence, invades another person's land or air space.

encumbrance   anything that affects or limits the title to a property, such as easements, leases, mortgages, or restrictions.

equity   the difference between the current market value of a property and the outstanding indebtedness due on it.

equity of redemption   the right of a borrower to stop the foreclosure process.

escalation clause   a clause in a lease allowing the lessor to charge more rent based on an increase in costs; sometimes called a pass-through clause.

escheat   the claim to property by the state when the owner dies intestate and no heirs can be found.

escrow   the deposit of funds and/or documents with a disinterested third party for safekeeping until the terms of the escrow agreement have been met.

escrow account   a trust account established to hold escrow funds for safekeeping until disbursement.

escrow analysis   annual report to disclose escrow receipts, payments, and current balances.

escrow disbursements   money paid from an escrow account.

estate   an interest in real property. The sum total of all the real property and personal property owned by an individual.

estate for years   a lease hold estate granting possession for a definite period of time.

estate tax   federal tax levied on property transferred upon death.

estoppel certificate   a document that certifies the outstanding amount owed on a mortgage loan, as well as the rate of interest.

et al.   abbreviation for the Latin phrase *et alius*, meaning "and another."

et ux.   abbreviation for Latin term *et uxor*, meaning "and wife."

et vir   Latin term meaning "and husband."

eviction   the lawful expulsion of an occupant from real property.

evidence of title   a document that identifies ownership of property.

examination of title   a review of an abstract to determine current condition of title.

exchange   a transaction in which property is traded for another property, rather than sold for money or other consideration.

exclusive agency listing   a contract between a property owner and one broker that only gives the broker the right to sell the property for a fee within a specified period of time but does not obligate the owner to pay the broker a fee if the owner produces his own buyer without the broker's assistance. The owner is barred only from appointing another broker within this time period.

execution   the signing of a contract.

executor/executrix   a person named in a will to administer an estate. The court will appoint an administrator if no executor is named. "Executrix" is the feminine form.

executory contract   a contract in which one or more of the obligations have yet to be performed.

executed contract   a contract in which all obligations have been fully performed.

express contract   an oral or written contract in which the terms are expressed in words.

extension agreement   an agreement between mortgagor and mortgagee to extend the maturity date of the mortgage after it is due.

F

fair market value   the highest price that a buyer, willing but not compelled to buy, would pay, and the lowest a seller, willing but not compelled to sell, would accept.

Fannie Mae   a congressionally chartered, privately owned corporation that is the nation's largest supplier of funds for home mortgages.

Federal Housing Administration (FHA)   an agency within the U.S. Department of Housing and Urban Development (HUD) that insures mortgage loans by FHA-approved lenders to make loans available to buyers with limited cash.

fee simple   most complete form of ownership of real estate.

FHA-insured loan   a loan insured by the Federal Housing Administration.

fiduciary relationship   a legal relationship with an obligation of trust, as that of agent and principal.

finder's fee   a fee or commission paid to a mortgage broker for finding a mortgage loan for a prospective borrower.

first mortgage   a mortgage that has priority to be satisfied over all other mortgages.

fixed-rate loan   a loan with an interest rate that does not change during the entire term of the loan.

fixture   an article of personal property that has been permanently attached to the real estate so as to become an integral part of the real estate.

foreclosure   the legal process by which a borrower in default of a mortgage is deprived of interest in the mortgaged property. Usually, this involves a forced sale of the property at public auction, where the proceeds of the sale are applied to the mortgage debt.

forfeiture the loss of money, property, rights, or privileges due to a breach of legal obligation.

franchise in real estate, an organization that lends a standardized trade name, operating procedures, referral services, and supplies to member brokerages.

fraud a deliberate misstatement of material fact or an act or omission made with deliberate intent to deceive (active fraud) or gross disregard for the truth (constructive fraud).

front foot a measurement of property taken by measuring the frontage of the property along the street line.

future interest ownership interest in property that cannot be enjoyed until the occurrence of some event; sometimes referred to as a household or equitable interest.

G

general agent an agent who is authorized to act for and obligate a principal in a specific range of matters, as specified by their mutual agreement.

general lien a claim on all property, real and personal, owned by a debtor.

government backed mortgage a mortgage that is insured by the Federal Housing Administration (FHA) or guaranteed by the Department of Veterans Affairs (VA) or the Rural Housing Service (RHS). Mortgages that are not government loans are identified as conventional loans.

Government National Mortgage Association (Ginnie Mae) a government-owned corporation within the U.S. Department of Housing and Urban Development (HUD). Ginnie Mae manages and liquidates government-backed loans and assists HUD in special lending projects.

government survey system   a method of land description in which meridians (lines of longitude) and base lines (lines of latitude) are used to divide land into townships and sections.

grant   the transfer of title to real property by deed.

grant deed   a deed that includes three warranties: (1) that the owner has the right to convey title to the property, (2) that there are no encumbrances other than those noted specifically in the deed, and (3) that the owner will convey any future interest that he or she may acquire in the property.

grantee   one who receives title to real property.

grantor   one who conveys title to real property; the present owner.

gross income multiplier   a rough method of estimating the market value of an income property by multiplying its gross annual rent by a multiplier discovered by dividing the sales price of comparable properties by their annual gross rent.

gross rent multiplier   similar to *gross income multiplier*, except that it looks at the relationship between sales price and monthly gross rent.

ground lease   a lease of land only on which a tenant already owns a building or will construct improvements.

guaranteed sale plan an agreement between a broker and a seller that the broker will buy the seller's property if it does not sell within a specified period of time.

H

hamlet a small village.

heir one who is legally entitled to receive property when the owner dies intestate.

highest and best use the legally permitted use of a parcel of land that will yield the greatest return to the owner in terms of money or amenities.

holdover tenancy a tenancy where a lessee retains possession of the property after the lease has expired, and the landlord, by continuing to accept rent, agrees to the tenant's continued occupancy.

home equity conversion mortgage (HECM) often called a reverse-annuity mortgage; instead of making payments to a lender, the lender makes payments to you. It enables older homeowners to convert the equity they have in their homes into cash, usually in the form of monthly payments. Unlike traditional home equity loans, a borrower does not qualify on the basis of income but on the value of his or her home. In addition, the loan does not have to be repaid until the borrower no longer occupies the property.

home equity line of credit a mortgage loan that allows the borrower to obtain cash drawn against the equity of his or her home, up to a predetermined amount.

home inspection a thorough inspection by a professional that evaluates the structural and mechanical condition of a property.

A satisfactory home inspection is often included as a contingency by the purchaser.

homestead   the parcel of land and improvements legally qualifying as the owner's principal residence.

I

implied contract   a contract where the agreement of the parties is created by their conduct.

improvement   human-made addition to real estate.

income capitalization approach   a method of estimating the value of income-producing property by dividing its expected annual net operating income of the property by a capitalization rate.

income property   real estate developed or improved to produce income.

independent contractor   one who is retained by another to perform a certain task and is not subject to the control and direction of the hiring person with regard to the end result of the task. Individual contractors receive a fee for their services, but pay their own expenses and taxes and receive no employee benefits.

index   a number used to compute the interest rate for an adjustable-rate mortgage (ARM). The index is a published number or percentage, such as the average yield on Treasury bills. A margin is added to the index to determine the interest rate to be charged on the ARM. This interest rate is subject to any caps that are associated with the mortgage.

inflation   an increase in the amount of money or credit available in relation to the amount of goods or services available, which causes an increase in the general price level of goods and services.

initial interest rate   the beginning interest rate of the mortgage at the time of closing. This rate changes for an adjustable-rate mortgage (ARM).

installment   the regular, periodic payment that a borrower agrees to make to a lender, usually related to a loan.

installment contract   see *contract for deed.*

installment loan   borrowed money that is repaid in periodic payments, known as installments.

installment sale   a transaction in which the sales price is paid to the seller in two or more installments over more than one calendar year.

insurance   a contract that provides indemnification from specific losses in exchange for a periodic payment. The individual contract is known as an insurance policy, and the periodic payment is known as an insurance premium.

insurance binder   a document that states that temporary insurance is in effect until a permanent insurance policy is issued.

insured mortgage   a mortgage that is protected by the Federal Housing Administration (FHA) or by private mortgage insurance (PMI). If the borrower defaults on the loan, the insurer must pay the lender the insured amount.

interest   a fee charged by a lender for the use of the money loaned; or a share of ownership in real estate.

interest accrual rate   the percentage rate at which interest accrues on the mortgage.

interest rate   the rent or rate charged to use funds belonging to another.

interest rate buydown plan   an arrangement where the property seller (or any other party) deposits money to an account so that it can be released each month to reduce the mortgagor's monthly payments during the early years of a mortgage. During the specified period, the mortgagor's effective interest rate is "bought down" below the actual interest rate.

interest rate ceiling   the maximum interest rate that may be charged for an adjustable-rate mortgage (ARM), as specified in the mortgage note.

interest rate floor   the minimum interest rate for an adjustable-rate mortgage (ARM), as specified in the mortgage note.

intestate   to die without having authored a valid will.

invalid   not legally binding or enforceable.

investment property   a property not occupied by the owner.

J

joint tenancy   co-ownership that gives each tenant equal interest and equal rights in the property, including the right of survivorship.

joint venture   an agreement between two or more parties to engage in a specific business enterprise.

judgment   a decision rendered by court determining the rights and obligations of parties to an action or lawsuit.

judgment lien   a lien on the property of a debtor resulting from a court judgment.

judicial foreclosure   a proceeding that is handled as a civil lawsuit and conducted through court; used in some states.

jumbo loan   a loan that exceeds Fannie Mae's mortgage amount limits. Also called a nonconforming loan.

junior mortgage   any mortgage that is inferior to a first lien and that will be satisfied only after the first mortgage; also called a secondary mortgage.

L

laches   a doctrine used by a court to bar the assertion of a legal claim or right, based on the failure to assert the claim in a timely manner.

land   The earth from its surface to its center of the earth, and the air space above it.

lease   a contract between a landlord and a tenant wherein the landlord grants the tenant possession and use of the property for a specified period of time and for a consideration.

leased fee   the landlord's interest in a parcel of leased property.

lease option   a financing option that allows homebuyers to lease a home with an option to buy. Each month's rent payment may consist of rent, plus an additional amount that can be applied toward the down payment on an already specified price.

leasehold a tenant's right to occupy a parcel of real estate for the term of a lease.

lessee the one who receives that right to use and occupy the property during the term of the leasehold estate.

lessor the owner of the property who grants the right of possession to the lessee.

leverage the use of borrowed funds to purchase an asset.

levy to assess or collect a tax.

license (1) a revocable authorization to perform a particular act on another's property, (2) authorization granted by a state to act as a real estate broker or salesperson.

lien a legal claim against a property to secure payment of a financial obligation.

life estate a freehold estate in real property limited in duration to the lifetime of the holder of the life estate or another specified person.

life tenant one who holds a life estate.

listing agreement a contract between the owner and a licensed real estate broker where the broker is employed to sell real estate on the owner's terms within a given time, for which service the owner agrees to pay the broker an agreed-upon fee.

listing broker a broker who contracts with a property owner to sell or lease the described property; the listing agreement typically may provide for the broker to make property available through a multiple listing system.

littoral rights   landowner's claim to use water in large, navigable lakes and oceans adjacent to property; ownership rights to land-bordering bodies of water up to the high-water mark.

loan   a sum of borrowed money, or principal, that is generally repaid with interest.

loan officer   or lender, serves several functions and has various responsibilities, such as soliciting loans; a loan officer both represents the lending institution and represents the borrower to the lending institution.

lock-in   an agreement in which the lender guarantees a specified interest rate for a certain amount of time.

lock-in period   the time period during which the lender has guaranteed an interest rate to a borrower.

M

margin   the difference between the interest rate and the index on an adjustable rate mortgage. The margin remains stable over the life of the loan, while the index fluctuates.

market data approach   a method of estimating the value of a property by comparing it to similar properties recently sold and making monetary adjustments for the differences between the subject property and the comparable property.

market value   the amount that a seller may expect to obtain for merchandise, services, or securities in the open market.

mechanic's lien   a statutory lien created to secure payment for those who supply labor or materials for the construction of an improvement to land.

metes and bounds   a method of describing a parcel of land using direction and distance.

mill   one-tenth of one cent; used by some states to express or calculate property tax rates.

modification   the act of changing any of the terms of the mortgage.

month-to-month tenancy   tenancy in which the tenant rents for only one month at a time.

mortgage   a written instrument that pledges property to secure payment of a debt obligation as evidenced by a promissory note. When duly recorded in the public record, a mortgage creates a lien against the title to a property.

mortgage banker   an entity that originates, funds, and services loans to be sold into the secondary money market.

mortgage broker   an entity that, for a fee, brings borrowers together with lenders.

mortgage lien   an encumbrance created by recording a mortgage.

mortgagee   the lender who benefits from the mortgage.

mortgagor   the borrower who pledges the property as collateral.

multidwelling units   properties that provide separate housing units for more than one family that secure only a single mortgage. Apartment buildings are also considered multidwelling units.

multiple listing system (MLS—also multiple listing service) method of marketing a property listing to all participants in the MLS.

N

negative amortization   occurs when an adjustable rate mortgage is allowed to fluctuate independently of a required minimum payment. A gradual increase in mortgage debt happens when the monthly payment is not large enough to cover the entire principal and interest due. The amount of the shortfall is added to the remaining balance to create negative amortization.

net listing   a listing in which the broker's fee is established as anything above a specified amount to be received by the seller from the sale of the property.

net worth   the value of all of a person's assets.

no cash-out refinance   a refinance transaction in which the new mortgage amount is limited to the sum of the remaining balance of the existing first mortgage

nonliquid asset   an asset that cannot easily be converted into cash.

note   a promise to repay an obligation; an "IOU" that defines how a loan will be repaid.

note rate   the interest rate on a promissory note.

notice of default   a formal written notice to a borrower that a default has occurred on a loan and that legal action may be taken.

nonconforming use a use of land that is permitted to continue, or grandfathered, even after a zoning ordinance is passed that prohibits the use.

notarize to attest or certify by a notary public.

novation the substitution of a new contract for an existing one; the new contract must reference the first and indicate that the first is being replaced and no longer has any force and effect.

O

obligee person on whose favor an obligation is entered.

obligor person who is bound to another by an obligation.

obsolescence a loss in the value of a property due to functional or external factors.

offer to propose as payment; bid on property.

offer and acceptance two of the necessary elements for the creation of a contract.

open-end mortgage a loan containing a clause that allows the mortgagor to borrow additional funds from the lender, up to a specified amount, without rewriting the mortgage.

option an agreement that gives a prospective buyer the right to purchase a seller's property within a specified period of time for a specified price.

optionee one who receives or holds an option.

optionor one who grants an option; the property owner.

ordinance a municipal regulation.

original principal balance   the total amount of principal owed on a loan before any payments are made; the amount borrowed.

origination fee   the amount charged by a lender to cover the cost of assembling the loan package and originating the loan.

owner financing   a real estate transaction in which the property seller provides all or part of the financing.

P

package mortgage   a mortgage that pledges both real and personal property as collateral to secure repayment of a loan.

parcel   a lot or specific portion of a large tract of real estate.

participation mortgage   a type of mortgage in which the lender receives a certain percentage of the income or resale proceeds from a property, as well as interest on the loan.

partnership   an agreement between two parties to conduct business for profit. In a partnership, property is owned by the partnership, not the individual partners, so partners cannot sell their interest in the property without the consent of the other partners.

payee   one who receives payment from another.

payor   one who makes payment to another.

percentage lease   a lease in which the rental rate is based on a percentage of the tenant's gross sales. This type of lease is most often used for retail space.

periodic estate   tenancy that automatically renews itself until either the landlord or tenant gives notice to terminate it.

personal property (heraditaments)　all items that are not permanently attached to real estate; also known as chattels.

physical deterioration　a loss in the value of a property due to impairment of its physical condition.

PITI　principal, interest, taxes, and insurance—components of a regular mortgage payment.

planned unit development (PUD)　a type of zoning that provides for residential and commercial uses within a specified area.

plat　a map of subdivided land showing the boundaries of individual parcels or lots.

plat number　a number that identifies a parcel of real estate for which a plat has been recorded in the public record.

PMI　private mortgage insurance.

point of beginning　the starting point for a survey using the "metes and bounds" method of description.

point　a point is one percent of the loan.

power of attorney　a legal document that authorizes someone to act on another's behalf. A power of attorney can grant complete authority or can be limited to certain acts and/or certain periods of time.

pre-approval　condition where a borrower has completed a loan application and provided debt, income, and savings documentation that an underwriter has reviewed and approved. A pre-approval is usually done at a certain loan amount, making assumptions about what the interest rate will actually be at the time the loan is actually made, as well as estimates for the amount that will be paid for property taxes, insurance, etc.

prepayment   amount paid to reduce the outstanding principal balance of a loan before the due date.

prepayment penalty   a fee charged to a borrower by a lender for paying off a debt before the term of the loan expires.

pre-qualification   a lender's opinion on the ability of a borrower to qualify for a loan, based on furnished information regarding debt, income, and available capital for down payment, closing costs, and pre-paids. Pre-qualification is less formal than **pre-approval**.

prescription   a method of acquiring an easement to property by prolonged, unauthorized use.

primary mortgage market   the financial market in which loans are originated, funded, and serviced.

prime rate   the short-term interest rate that banks charge to their preferred customers. Changes in prime rate are used as the indexes in some adjustable rate mortgages, such as home equity lines of credit.

principal   (1) one who authorizes another to act on his or her behalf, (2) one of the contracting parties to a transaction, (3) the amount of money borrowed in a loan, separate from the interest charged on it.

principal meridian   one of the 36 longitudinal lines used in the rectangular survey system method of land description.

probate   the judicial procedure of proving the validity of a will.

promissory note   details the terms of the loan and is the debt instrument.

property management   the operating of an income property for another.

property tax   a tax levied by the government on property, real or personal.

prorate   to divide ongoing property costs such as taxes or maintenance fees proportionately between buyer and seller at closing.

pur autre vie   a phrase meaning "for the life of another." In a life estate *pur autre vie*, the term of the estate is measured by the life of a person other than the person who holds the life estate.

purchase agreement   a written contract signed by the buyer and seller stating the terms and conditions under which a property will be sold.

purchase money mortgage   a mortgage given by a buyer to a seller to secure repayment of any loan used to pay part or all of the purchase price.

Q

qualifying ratios   calculations to determine whether a borrower can qualify for a mortgage. There are two ratios. The "top" ratio is a calculation of the borrower's monthly housing costs (principle, taxes, insurance, mortgage insurance, homeowner's association fees) as a percentage of monthly income. The "bottom" ratio includes housing costs as well as all other monthly debt.

quitclaim deed   conveyance where the grantor transfers without warranty or obligations whatever interest or title he/she may have.

R

real estate   land, the earth below it, the air above it, and anything permanently attached to it.

real estate agent   a real estate broker who has been appointed to market a property for and represent the property owner (listing agent), or a broker who has been appointed to represent the interest of the buyer (buyer's agent).

real estate board   Organization whose members are primarily comprised of real estate sales agents, brokers, and administrators.

real estate broker   a licensed person, association, partnership, or corporation who negotiates real estate transactions for others for a fee.

Real Estate Settlement Procedures Act (RESPA)   a consumer protection law that requires lenders to give borrowers advance notice of closing costs and prohibits certain abusive practices against buyers using federally related loans to purchase their homes.

real property   the rights of ownership to land and its improvements.

REALTOR®   A registered trademark for use by members of the National Association of REALTORS® and affiliated state and local associations.

recording   entering documents, such as deeds and mortgages, into the public record to give constructive notice.

rectangular survey system   a method of land description based on principal meridians (lines of longitude) and base lines (lines of latitude). Also called the government survey system.

redemption period   the statutory period of time during which an owner can reclaim foreclosed property by paying the debt owed plus court costs and other charges established by statute.

refinance transaction   the process of paying off one loan with the proceeds from a new loan using the same property as security or collateral.

release clause   a clause in a mortgage that releases a portion of the property upon payment of a portion of the loan.

remainder estate   a future interest in an estate that takes effect upon the termination of a life estate.

remaining balance   in a mortgage, the amount of principal that has not yet been repaid.

remaining term   the original amortization term minus the number of payments that have been applied to it.

rent   a periodic payment paid by a lessee to a landlord for the use and possession of leased property.

replacement cost   the estimated current cost to replace an asset similar or equivalent to the one being appraised.

reproduction cost   the cost of building an exact duplicate of a building at current prices.

restriction (restrict covenant)   a limitation on the way a property can be used.

reversion the return of interest or title to the grantor of a life estate.

reverse annuity mortgage homeowner receives monthly checks or lump sum with no repayment until property is sold. Usually an agreement between mortgagor and elderly homeowners.

revision a revised or new version, as in a contract.

right of egress (or ingress) the right to enter or leave designated premises.

right of first refusal the right of a person to have the first opportunity to purchase property before it is offered to anyone else.

right of redemption the statutory right to reclaim ownership of property after a foreclosure sale.

right of survivorship in joint tenancy, the right of survivors to acquire the interest of a deceased joint tenant.

S

safety clause a contract provision that provides a time period following expiration of a listing agreement, during which the agent will be compensated if there is a transaction with a buyer who was initially introduced to the property by the agent.

sale-leaseback transaction where the owner sells improved property, and, as part of the same transaction, signs a long-term lease to remain in possession of its premises, thus becoming the tenant of the new owner.

sales contract a contract between a buyer and a seller outlining the terms of the sale.

salesperson   one who is licensed to sell real estate in a given territory.

salvage value   the value of a property at the end of its economic life.

satisfaction   an instrument acknowledging that a debt has been paid in full.

second mortgage   a mortgage that is in less than first lien position; see *junior mortgage*.

section   as used in the rectangular survey system, an area of land measuring one square mile, or 640 acres.

secured loan   a loan that is backed by property or collateral.

security   property that is offered as collateral for a loan.

selling broker   the broker who secures a buyer for a listed property; the selling broker may be the listing agent, a subagent, or a buyer's agent.

servient tenement   a property on which an easement or right-of-way for an adjacent (dominant) property passes.

setback   the amount of space between the lot line and the building line, usually established by a local zoning ordinance or restrictive covenants (deed restrictions).

settlement statement (HUD-1)   the form used to itemize all costs related to closing of a residential transaction covered by RESPA regulations.

severalty   the ownership of a property by only one legal entity.

special assessment a tax levied against only the specific properties that will benefit from a public improvement, such as a street or sewer; an assessment by a homeowners' association for a capital improvement to the common areas for which no budgeted funds are available.

special warranty deed a deed in which the grantor guarantees the title only against the defects that may have occurred during the grantor's ownership, and not against any defects that occurred prior to that time.

specific lien a lien, such as a mortgage, that attaches to one defined parcel of real estate.

standard payment calculation method used to calculate the monthly payment required to repay the remaining balance of a mortgage in equal installments over the remaining term of the mortgage at the current interest rate.

straight-line depreciation a method of computing depreciation by decreasing value by an equal amount each year during the useful life of the property.

statutory lien lien imposed on property by statute, such as a tax lien.

subdivision a tract of land divided into lots as defined in a publicly recorded plat that complies with state and local regulations.

sublet the act of a lessee transferring part or all of his or her lease to a third party while maintaining responsibility for all duties and obligations of the lease contract.

subordinate by contract, voluntarily accept a lower priority lien position than that to which one would normally be entitled.

substitution　　the principle in appraising that a buyer will be willing to pay no more for the property being appraised than the cost of purchasing an equally desirable property.

subrogation　　the substitution of one party into another's legal role as the creditor for a particular debt.

suit for possession　　a lawsuit filed by a landlord to evict a tenant who has violated the terms of the lease or retained possession of the property after the lease expired.

survey　　a map that shows the exact legal boundaries of a property, the location of easements, encroachments, improvements, rights of way, and other physical features.

T

tax deed　　instrument given to purchaser at time of sale in some states.

tax lien　　a charge against a property created by law or statue; tax liens take priority over all other types of liens.

tax rate　　the rate applied to the assessed value of a property to determine the property taxes.

tax sale　　the court-ordered sale of a property after the owner fails to pay advalorem taxes owed on the property.

tenancy at sufferance　　the tenancy of a party who unlawfully retains possession of a landlord's property after the term of the lease has expired.

tenancy at will　　an indefinite tenancy that can be terminated by either the landlord or the tenant at any time by giving notice to the other party one rental period in advance of the desired termination date.

tenancy by the entirety ownership by a married couple of property acquired during the marriage with right of survivorship; not recognized by community property states.

tenancy in common a form of co-ownership in which two or more persons hold an undivided interest in property without the right of survivorship.

tenant one who holds or possesses the right of occupancy title.

tenement space that may be occupied by a tenant under the terms of a lease.

testate to die having created a valid will directing the testator's desires with regard to the disposition of the estate.

timesharing undivided ownership of real estate for only an allotted portion of a year.

title a legal document that demonstrates a person's right to, or ownership of, a property. Note: title is *not* an instrument. The instrument such as a deed gives evidence of title or ownership.

title insurance an insurance policy that protects the holder from defects in a title, subject to the exceptions noted in the policy.

title search a check of public records to ensure that the seller is the legal owner of the property and that there are no liens or other outstanding claims.

Torrens system a system of registering titles to land with a public authority, who is usually called a registrar.

township a division of land, measuring six miles square (36 square miles), in the government survey system.

transfer tax state or municipal tax payable when the conveyancing instrument is recorded.

trust an arrangement in which title to property is transferred from a grantor to a trustee, who holds title but not the right of possession for a third party, the beneficiary.

trustee A person who holds title to property for another person designated as the beneficiary.

truth in lending law also known as Regulation Z; requires lenders to make full disclosure regarding the terms of a loan.

U

underwriting the process of evaluating a loan application to determine the risk involved for the lender.

undivided interest the interest of co-owners to use of an entire property despite the fractional interest owned.

unilateral contract a one-sided contract in which one party is obligated to perform a particular act completely, before the other party has any obligation to perform.

unsecured loan a loan that is not backed by collateral or security.

useful life the period of time a property is expected to have economic utility.

usury the practice of charging interest at a rate higher than that allowed by law.

V

VA-guaranteed loan   a mortgage loan made to a qualified veteran that is guaranteed by the Department of Veterans Affairs.

valid contract   an agreement that is legally enforceable and binding on all parties.

valuation   estimated worth.

variance   permission obtained from zoning authorities to build a structure that is not in complete compliance with current zoning laws. A variance does not permit a non-conforming use of a property.

vendee   a buyer.

vendor   a seller; the property owner.

village   an incorporated minor municipality usually larger than a hamlet and smaller than a town.

void contract   a contract that is not legally enforceable; the absence of a valid contract.

voidable contract   contract that appears to be valid but is subject to cancellation by one or both of the parties.

W

waiver   the surrender of a known right or claim.

warranty deed   a deed in which the grantor fully warrants a good clear title to the property.

will   a written document that directs the distribution of a deceased person's property, real and personal.

wraparound mortgage   a mortgage that includes the remaining balance on an existing first mortgage plus an additional amount. Full payments on both mortgages are made to the wraparound mortgagee who then forwards the payments on the first mortgage to the first mortgagee.

Z

zone   an area reserved by authorities for specific use that is subject to certain restrictions.

zoning ordinance   the exercise of regulating and controlling the use of a property in a municipality.

Appendix

SELECTED ASSOCIATIONS

These real estate organizations provide support or services that you may find useful as you embark on your real estate career. This list includes real estate trade groups as well as related services, such as appraisers, home inspectors, lenders, and relocation services. At press time, these websites were current, but due to the ever-changing nature of the Web, some of these addresses may no longer be in service.

Accolade Network, Inc. (real estate appraiser network)
National Assignment Center
415 G Street
Modesto, CA 95351
209-522-9981
www.appraise.com

American Industrial Real Estate Association
700 S. Flower, Suite 600
Los Angeles, CA 90017
213-687-8777
www.airea.com

American Land Title Association
1828 L Street NW, Suite 705
Washington, DC 20036
202-296-3671
www.alta.org

American Planning Association
122 S. Michigan Avenue, Suite 1600
Chicago, IL 60603-6107
312-431-9100
www.planning.org

The American Real Estate Society (ARES)
College of Business & Public Administration
Gamble Hall, Room 160A
University of North Dakota
P.O. Box 7120
Grand Forks, ND 58202-7120
701-777-3670
www.aresnet.org

American Society of Appraisers
555 Herndon Parkway, Suite 125
Herndon, VA 20170
703-478-2228
www.appraisers.org

American Society of Farm Managers and Rural Appraisers
950 S. Cherry Street, Suite 508
Denver, CO 80246
303-758-3513
www.asfmra.org

American Society of Home Inspectors
932 Lee Street, Suite 101
Des Plaines IL 60016-6546
800-743-ASHI
www.ashi.com

The Appraisal Foundation
1029 Vermont Avenue NW, Suite 900
Washington, DC 20005-3517
202-347-7722
www.appraisalfoundation.org

Appraisal Institute
875 N. Michigan Avenue, Suite 2400
Chicago, IL 60611-1980
312-335-4100
www.appraisalinstitute.org

Building Owners and Managers Association International
1201 New York Avenue NW, Suite 300
Washington, DC 20005
202-408-2662
www.boma.org

Commercial Investment Real Estate Institute
430 N. Michigan Avenue
Chicago, IL 60611
800-621-7027
www.ccim.com

Employee Relocation Council
1720 N Street NW
Washington, DC 20036
202-857-0857
www.erc.org

Environmental Systems Research Institute, Inc. (GIS &
mapping services)
380 New York Street
Redlands, CA 92373-8100
800-447-9778
www.esri.com

Home Inspections—USA Home Inspection Directory Corp.
P.O. Box 255
West Ossipee, NH 03890
877-491-2171
www.homeinspections-usa.com/contact.html

Inman Real Estate News
1250 45th Street, Suite 360
Emeryville, CA 94608
800-775-4662
www.inman.com

Institute of Real Estate Management
430 N. Michigan Avenue
Chicago, IL 60611-4090
800-837-0706
www.irem.org

Mortgage Bankers Association of America
1125 15th Street NW
Washington, DC 20005
202-861-6500
www.mbaa.org

National Association of Home Builders
1201 15th Street NW
Washington, DC 20005
202-822-0200
www.nahb.com

National Association of Home Inspectors
4248 Park Glen Road
Minneapolis, MN 55416
800-448-3942
www.nahi.org

National Association of Independent Fee Appraisers
7501 Murdoch Avenue
St. Louis, MO 63119
314-781-6688
www.naifa.com

National Association of Master Appraisers
303 W. Cypress Street
San Antonio, TX 78212-0617
800-229-6262
www.masterappraisers.com

National Association of Mortgage Brokers
8201 Greensboro Drive, Suite 300
McLean, VA 22102
703-610-9009
www.namb.org

National Association of Real Estate Editors
1003 N.W. 6th Terrace
Boca Raton, FL 33486
www.naree.org

National Association of Real Estate Appraisers
1224 North Nokomis N.E.
Alexandria, MN 56308
320-763-7626
www.iami.org/narea.cfm

National Association of Real Estate Brokers
1629 K Street, NW, Suite 602
Washington, DC 20006
202-785-4477
www.nareb.com

National Association of REALTORS®
430 N. Michigan Avenue
Chicago, IL 60611
312-329-8200
www.realtor.com

National Association of Residential Property Managers
6300 Dutchman's Parkway
Louisville, KY 40205
800-782-3452
www.narpm.org

National Property Management Association
The Oaktree Center, 1108 Pinehurst Road
Dunedin, FL 34698
727-736-3788
www.npma.org

Council of Real Estate Brokerage Managers Council
430 N. Michigan Avenue
Chicago, IL 60611-4092
800-621-8738
www.crb.com

Read Estate Educators Association
320 West Sabal Palm Place, Suite 150
Longwood, FL 32779
407-834-6688
www.reea.org

Realty Times
5600 W. Lovers Lane, Suite 315
Dallas, TX 75209
214-353-6980
www.realtimes.com

Women's Council of REALTORS®
430 N. Michigan Avenue
Chicago, IL 60611
312-329-8483
www.wcr.org